5/22/10

To: Annie ~

The one person in
this world who will
truly relish this book

Love,
Mom & Daddy

MFK FISHER

An Alphabet for Gourmets

NORTH POINT PRESS
Farrar, Straus and Giroux
New York

North Point Press
A division of Farrar, Straus and Giroux
19 Union Square West, New York 10003

Copyright © 1949, 1954 by M.F.K. Fisher
All rights reserved
Distributed in Canada by Douglas & McIntyre Ltd.
Printed in the United States of America
Originally published in 1949 by Viking Press
This edition first published in 1989 by North Point Press

LIBRARY OF CONGRESS CATALOGING-IN-PUBLICATION DATA
Fisher, M.F.K. (Mary Frances Kennedy), 1908–1992
    An alphabet for gourmets / M.F.K. Fisher
        p.   cm.
      ISBN-13: 978-0-86547-391-1 (alk. paper)
      ISBN-10: 0-86547-391-9
    Reprint. Originally published: New York: Viking Press, 1949.
    Includes index.
    1. Gastronomy.   I. Title.
TX633.F5 1989   641.'01'3—dc19   88-32966

Designed by David Bullen

www.fsgbooks.com

16   15   14   13   12   11   10   9

For Hal Bieler, who has taught me
more than he meant to about
the pleasures of the table

Contents

Foreword

It is apparently impossible for me to say anything about gastronomy, the art and science of satisfying one of our three basic human needs, without involving myself in what might be called side issues—might be, that is, by anyone who does not believe, as I do, that it is futile to consider hunger as a thing separate from people who are hungry.

That is why, when I set myself to follow anything as seemingly arbitrary as an alphabet, with its honored and unchanging sequence and its firm count of twenty-six letters, I must keep myself well in hand lest I find *A Is for Apple*, *B Is for Borscht*, and *C Is for Codfish Cakes* turning into one novel, one political diatribe, and one nonfiction book on the strange love-makings of sea monsters, each written largely in terms of eating, drinking, digesting, and each written by *me*, shaped, molded, and, to some minds, distorted by my own vision, which depends in turn on my state of health, passion, finances, and my general glandular balance.

If a woman can be made more peaceful, a man fuller and richer, children happier, by a changed approach to the basically brutish satisfaction of hunger, why should not I, the person who brought about that change, feel a definite and rewarding urge to proselytize? If a young man can learn to woo with cup and spoon as well as his inborn virility, why should not I who showed him how feel myself among Gasterea's anointed? The possibilities for bettering the somewhat dingy patterns of life on earth by a new interest in how best to stay our human hunger are so infinite that, to my mind at least, some such tyrannical limitations as an ABC will impose are almost requisite.

The alphabet is also controversial, which in itself is good. Why, someone may ask, did I scamp such lush fields as *L Is for Lucullus*, *G Is for Gourmet*? Why did I end the alphabet with a discussion of the hors d'oeuvres called zakuski, surely more appropriate at the beginning of any feast, literary or otherwise, and ignore the fine fancies to be evoked by the word zabaglione, with all its connotations of sweet satisfaction and high flavor?

I do not really know, but most probably because I am myself. This ABC is the way *I* wrote it. There is room between its lines, and even its words, for each man to write his own gastronomical beliefs, call forth his own remembered feastings, and taste once more upon his mind's tongue the wine and the clear rock-water of cups uncountable.

An Alphabet
for Gourmets

A *is for*
dining Alone

. . . and so am I, if a choice must be made between most people I know and myself. This misanthropic attitude is one I am not proud of, but it is firmly there, based on my increasing conviction that sharing food with another human being is an intimate act that should not be indulged in lightly.

There are few people alive with whom I care to pray, sleep, dance, sing, or share my bread and wine. Of course there are times when this latter cannot be avoided if we are to exist socially, but it is endurable only because it need not be the only fashion of self-nourishment.

There is always the cheering prospect of a quiet or giddy or warmly somber or lightly notable meal with "One," as Elizabeth Robins Pennell refers to him or her in *The Feasts of Autolycus*. "*One* sits at your side feasting in silent sympathy," this lady wrote at the end of the last century in her mannered and delightful book. She was, at this point, thinking of eating an orange[1] in southern Europe, but any kind of food will do, in any clime, so long as *One* is there.

I myself have been blessed among women in this respect—

which is of course the main reason that, if *One* is not there, dining alone is generally preferable to any other way for me.

Naturally there have been times when my self-made solitude has irked me. I have often eaten an egg and drunk a glass of jug-wine, surrounded deliberately with the trappings of busyness, in a hollow Hollywood flat near the studio where I was called a writer, and not been able to stifle my longing to be anywhere but there, in the company of any of a dozen predatory or ambitious or even kind people who had *not* invited me.

That was the trouble: nobody did.

I cannot pretend, even on an invisible black couch of day-dreams, that I have ever been hounded by Sunset Boulevardiers who wanted to woo me with caviar and win me with Pol Roger; but in my few desolate periods of being without *One* I have known two or three avuncular gentlemen with a latent gleam in their eyes who understood how to order a good mixed grill with watercress. But, for the most part, to the lasting shame of my female vanity, they have shied away from any suggestion that we might dally, gastronomically speaking. "Wouldn't dare ask *you*," they have murmured, shifting their gaze with no apparent difficulty or regret to some much younger and prettier woman who had never read a recipe in her life, much less written one, and who was for that very reason far better fed than I.

It has for too long been the same with the ambitious eaters, the amateur chefs and the self-styled gourmets, the leading lights of food-and-wine societies. When we meet, in other people's houses or in restaurants, they tell me a few sacrosanct and impressive details of how they baste grouse with truffle juice, then murmur, "Wouldn't dare serve it to *you*, of course," and forthwith invite some visiting potentate from Nebraska, who never saw a truffle in his life, to register the proper awe in return for a Lucullan and perhaps delicious meal.[2]

And the kind people—they are the ones who have made me feel the loneliest. Wherever I have lived, they have indeed been kind—up to a certain point. They have poured cocktails for me, and praised me generously for things I have written to their liking, and showed me their children. And I have seen the discreetly drawn curtains to their family dining rooms, so different from the uncluttered, spinsterish emptiness of my own one room. Behind the far door to the kitchen I have sensed, with the mystic materialism of a hungry woman, the presence of honest-to-God fried chops, peas and carrots, a jello salad,[3] and lemon meringue pie—none of which I like and all of which I admire in theory and would give my eyeteeth to be offered. But the kind people always murmur, "We'd love to have you stay to supper sometime. We wouldn't *dare*, of course, the simple way we eat and all."

As I leave, by myself, two nice plump kind neighbors come in. They say howdo, and then good-by with obvious relief, after a polite, respectful mention of culinary literature as represented, no matter how doubtfully, by me. They sniff the fine creeping straightforward smells in the hall and living room, with silent thanks that they are not condemned to my daily fare of quails financière, pâté de Strasbourg truffé en brioche, sole Marguéry, bombe vanille au Cointreau. They close the door on me.

I drive home by way of the corner Thriftimart to pick up another box of Ry Krisp, which with a can of tomato soup and a glass of California sherry will make a good nourishing meal for me as as I sit on my tuffet in a circle of proofs and pocket detective stories.

It took me several years of such periods of being alone to learn how to care for myself, at least at table. I came to believe that since nobody else dared feed me as I wished to be fed, I must do it myself, and with as much aplomb as I could muster.

Enough of hit-or-miss suppers of tinned soup and boxed biscuits and an occasional egg just because I had failed once more to rate an invitation!

I resolved to establish myself as a well-behaved female at one or two good restaurants, where I could dine alone at a pleasant table with adequate attentions rather than be pushed into a corner and given a raw or overweary waiter. To my credit, I managed to carry out this resolution, at least to the point where two headwaiters accepted me: they knew I tipped well, they knew I wanted simple but excellent menus, and, above all, they knew that I could order and drink, all by myself, an apéritif and a small bottle of wine or a mug of ale, without turning into a maudlin, potential pick-up for the Gentlemen at the Bar.

Once or twice a week I would go to one of these restaurants and with carefully disguised self-consciousness would order my meal, taking heed to have things that would nourish me thoroughly as well as agreeably, to make up for the nights ahead when soup and crackers would be my fare. I met some interesting waiters: I continue to agree with a modern Mrs. Malaprop who said, "They are *so* much nicer than people!"

My expensive little dinners, however, became, in spite of my good intentions, no more than a routine prescription for existence. I had long believed that, once having bowed to the inevitability of the dictum that we must eat to live, we should ignore it and live to eat, in proportion of course. And there I was, spending more money than I should, on a grim plan which became increasingly complicated. In spite of the loyalty of my waiter friends, wolves in a dozen different kinds of sheep's clothing—from the normally lecherous to the Lesbian—sniffed at the high wall of my isolation. I changed seats, then tables. I read—I read everything from *Tropic of Cancer* to *Riders of the Purple Sage*. Finally I began to look around the room and hum.

That was when I decided that my own walk-up flat, my own script-cluttered room with the let-down bed, was the place for me. "Never be daunted in public" was an early Hemingway phrase that had more than once bolstered me in my timid twenties. I changed it resolutely to "Never be daunted in private."

I rearranged my schedule, so that I could market on my way to the studio each morning. The more perishable tidbits I hid in the watercooler just outside my office, instead of dashing to an all-night grocery for tins of this and that at the end of a long day. I bought things that would adapt themselves artfully to an electric chafing dish: cans of shad roe (a good solitary dish, since I always feel that nobody really likes it but me), consommé double, and such. I grew deliberately fastidious about eggs and butter; the biggest, brownest eggs were none too good, nor could any butter be too clover-fresh and sweet. I laid in a case or two of "unpretentious but delightful little wines." I was determined about the whole thing, which in itself is a great drawback emotionally. But I knew no alternative.

I ate very well indeed. I liked it too—at least more than I had liked my former can-openings or my elaborate preparations for dining out. I treated myself fairly dispassionately as a marketable thing, at least from ten to six daily, in a Hollywood studio story department, and I fed myself to maintain top efficiency. I recognized the dull facts that certain foods affected me this way, others that way. I tried to apply what I knew of proteins and so forth to my own chemical pattern, and I deliberately scrambled two eggs in a little sweet butter when quite often I would have liked a glass of sherry and a hot bath and to hell with food.

I almost never ate meat, mainly because I did not miss it and secondarily because it was inconvenient to cook on a little grill and to cut upon a plate balanced on my knee. Also, it made the one-room apartment smell. I invented a great many different salads, of fresh lettuces and herbs and vegetables, of marinated tinned vegetables, now and then of crabmeat and the like. I learned a few tricks to play on canned soups, and Escoffier as well as the Chinese would be astonished at what I did with beef bouillon and a handful of watercress or a teaspoonful of soy.

I always ate slowly, from a big tray set with a mixture of Woolworth and Spode; and I soothed my spirits beforehand with a glass of sherry or vermouth, subscribing to the ancient truth that only a relaxed throat can make a swallow. More often than not I drank a glass or two of light wine with the hot food: a big bowl of soup, with a fine pear and some Teleme Jack cheese; or two very round eggs, from a misnamed "poacher," on sourdough toast with browned butter poured over and a celery heart alongside for something crisp; or a can of bean sprouts, tossed with sweet butter and some soy and lemon juice, and a big glass of milk.

Things tasted good, and it was a relief to be away from my job and from the curious disbelieving impertinence of the people in restaurants. I still wished, in what was almost a theoretical way, that I was not cut off from the world's trenchermen by what I had written for and about them. But, and there was no cavil here, I felt firmly then, as I do this very minute, that snug misanthropic solitude is better than hit-or-miss congeniality. If *One* could not be with me, "feasting in silent sympathy," then I was my best companion.

I

Probably the best way to eat an orange is to pick it dead-ripe from the tree, bite into it once to start the peeling, and after peeling eat a section at a time.

Some children like to stick a hollow pencil of sugarcandy through a little hole into the heart of an orange and suck at it. I never did.

Under the high-glassed Galeria Vittorio Emanuele in Milan

before the bombs fell, the headwaiters of the two fine restaurants would peel an orange at your table with breath-taking skill and speed, slice it thin enough to see through, and serve it to you doused to your own taste with powdered sugar and any of a hundred liquors.

In this country Ambrosia is a dessert as traditionally and irrefutably Southern as pecan pie. My mother used to tell me how fresh and good it tasted, and how pretty it was, when she went to school in Virginia, a refugee from Iowa's dearth of proper *fin de siècle* finishing schools. I always thought of it as old-fashioned, as something probably unheard-of by today's bourbons. I discovered only lately that an easy way to raise an unladylike babble of protest is to say as much in a group of Confederate Daughters—and here is the proof, straight from one of their mouths, that their local gods still sup on

Ambrosia

6 *fine oranges*	1 ½ *cups sugar*
1 ½ *cups grated coconut,*	*good sherry*
preferably fresh	

Divide peeled oranges carefully into sections, or slice thin, and arrange in layers in a glass bowl, sprinkling each layer generously with sugar and coconut. When the bowl is full, pour a wine glass or so of sherry over the layers and chill well.

2

Crêpes, approximately Suzette, are the amateur gourmet's delight, and more elaborately sogged pancakes have been paddled about in more horrendous combinations of butter, fruit juices, and ill-assorted liqueurs in the name of gastronomy than it is well to think on.

A good solution to this urge to stand up at the end of a meal and flourish forks over a specially constructed chafing dish is to introduce local Amphytrions to some such simple elegance as the following, a recipe that was handed out free, fifteen years ago in France, by the company that made Grand Marnier:

> *Dissolve 3 lumps of sugar in 1 teaspoon of water. Add the zest of an orange, sweet butter the size of a walnut, and a liqueur glass of Grand Marnier. Heat quickly, pour over hot, rolled crêpes, set aflame, and serve.*

3

The following dish has almost the same simplicity as the preceding ones, but where they are excellent, this is, to my mind, purely horrible.

It is based on a packaged gelatin mixture which is almost a staple food in America. To be at its worst, which is easy, this should be pink, with imitation and also packaged whipped milk on top. To maintain this gastronomical level, it should be served in "salad" form, a small quivering slab upon a wilted lettuce leaf, with some such boiled dressing as the one made from the rule my maternal grandmother handed down to me, written in her elegantly spiderish script.

I can think of no pressure strong enough to force me to disclose, professionally, her horrid and austere receipt. Suffice it to say that it succeeds in producing, infallibly, a kind of sour, pale custard, blandly heightened by stingy pinches of mustard and salt, and made palatable to the most senile tongues by large amounts of sugar and flour and good water. Grandmother had little truck with foreign luxuries like olive oil, and while she thought nothing of having the cook make a twelve-egg cake every Saturday, she could not bring herself to use more than the required one egg in any such frippery as a salad dressing. The truth probably is that salads themselves were suspect in her culinary pattern, a grudging concession to the Modern Age.

B *is for*
Bachelors

. . . and the wonderful dinners they pull out of their cupboards with such dining room aplomb and kitchen chaos.

Their approach to gastronomy is basically sexual, since few of them under seventy-nine will bother to produce a good meal unless it is for a pretty woman. Few of them at any age will consciously ponder on the aphrodisiac qualities of the dishes they serve forth, but subconsciously they use what tricks they have to make their little banquets, whether intimate or merely convivial, lead as subtly as possible to the hoped-for bedding down.

Soft lights, plenty of tipples (from champagne to straight rye), and if possible a little music, are the timeworn props in any such entertainment, on no matter what financial level the host is operating. Some men head for the back booth at the corner pub and play the jukebox, with overtones of medium-rare steak and French fried potatoes. Others are forced to fall back on the soft-footed alcoholic ministrations of a Filipino houseboy, muted Stan Kenton on the super-Capeheart, and a little supper beginning with caviar malossol on ice and ending with a soufflé au kirschwasser d'Alsace.

The bachelors I'm considering at this moment are at neither end of the gastronomical scale. They are the men between twenty-five and fifty who if they have been married are temporarily out of it and are therefore triply conscious of both their heaven-sent freedom and their domestic clumsiness. They are in the middle brackets, financially if not emotionally. They have been around and know the niceties or amenities or whatever they choose to call the tricks of a well-set table and a well-poured glass, and yet they have neither the tastes nor the pocketbooks to indulge in signing endless chits at Mike Romanoff's or "21."

In other words, they like to give a little dinner now and again in the far from circumspect intimacy of their apartments, which more often than not consist of a studio–living room with either a disguised let-down bed or a tiny bedroom, a bath, and a stuffy closet called the kitchen.

I have eaten many meals prepared and served in such surroundings. I am perhaps fortunate to be able to say that I have always enjoyed them—and perhaps even more fortunate to be able to say that I enjoyed them because of my acquired knowledge of the basic rules of seduction. I assumed that I had been invited for either a direct or an indirect approach. I judged as best I could which one was being contemplated, let my host know of my own foreknowledge, and then sat back to have as much pleasure as possible.

I almost always found that since my host knew I was aware of the situation, he was more relaxed and philosophical about its very improbable outcome and could listen to the phonograph records and savor his cautiously concocted Martini with more inner calm. And I almost always ate and drank well, finding that any man who knows that a woman will behave in her cups, whether of consommé double or of double Scotch, is resigned happily to a good dinner; in fact, given the choice between it and a rousing tumble in the hay, he will inevitably choose the first, being convinced that the latter can perforce be found elsewhere.

The drinks offered to me were easy ones, dictated by my statements made early in the game (I never bothered to hint but always said plainly, in self-protection, that I liked very dry Gibsons with good ale to follow, or dry sherry with good wine: safe but happy, that was my motto). I was given some beautiful liquids: really old Scotch, Swiss Dézelay light as mountain water, proud vintage Burgundies, countless bottles of champagne, all good too, and what fine cognacs! Only once did a professional bachelor ever offer me a glass of sweet liqueur. I never saw him again, feeling that his perceptions were too dull for me to exhaust myself, if after even the short time needed to win my acceptance of his dinner invitation he had not guessed my tastes that far.

The dishes I have eaten at such tables-for-two range from homegrown snails in homemade butter to pompano flown in from the Gulf of Mexico with slivered macadamias from Maui—or is it Oahu? I have found that most bachelors like the exotic, at least culinarily speaking: they would rather fuss around with a complex recipe for Le Hochepot de Queue de Boeuf than with a simple one called Stewed Oxtail, even if both come from André Simon's *Concise Encyclopædia of Gastronomy*.[1]

They are snobs in that they prefer to keep Escoffier on the front of the shelf and hide Mrs. Kander's *Settlement Cook Book*.

They are experts at the casual: they may quit the office early and make a murderous sacrifice of pay, but when you arrive the apartment is pleasantly odorous, glasses and a perfectly frosted shaker or a bottle await you. Your host looks not even faintly harried or stovebound. His upper lip is unbedewed and his eye is flatteringly wolfish.

Tact and honest common sense forbid any woman's penetrating with mistaken kindliness into the kitchen: motherliness is unthinkable in such a situation, and romance would wither on the culinary threshold and be buried forever beneath its confusion of used pots and spoons.

Instead the time has come for ancient and always interesting blandishments, of course in proper proportions. The Bachelor Spirit unfolds like a hungry sea anemone. The possible object of his affections feels cozily desired. The drink is good. He pops discreetly in and out of his gastronomical workshop, where he brews his sly receipts, his digestive attacks upon the fortress of her virtue. She represses her natural curiosity, and if she is at all experienced in such wars she knows fairly well that she will have a patterned meal which has already been indicated by his ordering in restaurants. More often than not it will be some kind of chicken, elaborately disguised with everything from Australian pine nuts to herbs grown by the landlady's daughter.

One highly expert bachelor-cook in my immediate circle swears by a recipe for breasts of young chicken, poached that morning or the night before, and covered with a dramatic and very lemony sauce made at the last minute in a chafing dish. This combines all the tricks of seeming nonchalance, carefully casual presentation, and attention-getting.

With it he serves chilled asparagus tips in his own version of vinaigrette sauce and little hot rolls. For dessert he has what is also his own version of riz à l'Impératrice, which he is convinced all women love because he himself secretly dotes on it—and it can be made the day before, though not too successfully.

This meal lends itself almost treacherously to the wiles of alcohol: anything from a light lager to a Moët et Chandon of a great year is beautiful with it, and can be well bolstered with the preprandial drinks which any bachelor doles out with at least one ear on the Shakespearean dictum that they may double desire and halve the pursuit thereof.

The most successful bachelor dinner I was ever plied with, or perhaps it would be more genteel to say served, was also thoroughly horrible.

Everything was carried out, as well as in, by a real expert, a man then married for the fifth time who had interspersed his connubial adventures with rich periods of technical celibacy. The cocktails were delicately suited to my own tastes rather than his, and I sipped a glass of Tio Pepe, properly chilled. The table, set in a candle-lit patio, was laid in the best sense of the word "nicely," with silver and china and Swedish glass which I had long admired. The wine was a last bottle of Chianti, " *'stra vecchio.*"

We ate thin strips of veal that had been dipped in an artful mixture of grated Parmesan and crumbs, with one of the bachelor's favorite tricks to accompany it, buttered thin noodles gratinés with extra-thin and almond-brown toasted noodles on top. There was a green salad.

The night was full of stars, and so seemed my eager host's brown eyes, and the whole thing was ghastly for two reasons: he had forgotten to take the weather into his menu planning, so that we were faced with a rich, hot, basically heavy meal on one of the worst summer nights in local history, and I was at the queasiest possible moment of pregnancy.

Of course the main mistake was in his trying to entertain a woman in that condition as if she were still seduceable and/or he still a bachelor: we had already been married several months.

I

Two of the three proper recipes in Monsieur Simon's useful as well as delightful volume on meat in his *Concise Encyclopædia of Gastronomy* recommend soaking the sections of ox tail in either hot or cold water. For oxtail soup this is a good idea, but I myself do not like it for stew because it robs the texture of that almost glutinous thickness which should be one of its chief characteristics, and which when correctly brought about should obviate the use of flour in thickening its ample gravy. (I say this humbly but positively.)

One of the three recipes in Simon's *Meat*, typical in all its practical common sense of the *farmhouse fare* from which it is culled, says in italics something that wins my heart and my approval, something true of every kind of stew I ever made: *"It is always better to start cooking this dish a day before it is wanted."*

Here is my recipe, subject to unbasic change of course, following the season and the vegetables thereof:

Oxtail Stew

3 *ox tails, cut in joints and discarding the smallest ends*	8 *or 10 small peeled onions*
3 *tablespoons butter*	8 *or 10 peeled potatoes*
3 *tablespoons olive oil (or bacon fat)*	1 *small bunch celery, with its leaves, in 1-inch pieces*
salt, pepper, bay leaf, what you will	6 *or 8 thickly sliced carrots handful of chopped parsley*
1 *quart (or more to taste) of either tinned consommé, stock, vegetable juice, or even beef cubes in water*	1 *clove chopped garlic*
	6 *chopped peeled fresh tomatoes (or 1 No. 2 can)*

Brown the clean oxtail joints in the melted butter and fat. Season. Add the stock. Cover tightly and let simmer until tender, adding the vegetables for the last 40 to 60 minutes of cooking. (Pressure-cooked vegetables with their juices can be added when the meat is completely done.) Mix well, put to one side, and serve the next day, first tasting to "rectify," as some cooks say. Seasonings and texture will have set, and red wine, more salt, even a judicious thickening may seem necessary.

C is for
Cautious

. . . the kind of dinner at which there is an undercurrent of earnest timidity, of well-meant and badly directed eagerness to do well, and absolutely no true feeling for what can best be described as Fun at Table.

A complete lack of caution is perhaps one of the true signs of a real gourmet: he has no need for it, being filled as he is with a God-given and intelligently self-cultivated sense of gastronomical freedom. He not only knows from everything admirable he has read that he will not like Irish whisky with pineapple chilled in honey and vermouth, or a vintage Chambertin with poached lake perch; but every taste bud on both his actual and his spiritual palate wilts in revulsion at such thoughts. He does not serve these or similar combinations, not because he has been *told*, but because he *knows*.

But there are some would-be gastronomers who live only by the book. Most of them are happily unconscious of their loss. Many of them acquire a basic knowledge of the pleasures of the table that is often astonishingly broad, and that gives them countless fine moments of generosity and well-being: what is much better in life than to be hospitable and to know by your guests' faces that you have proved a noble host indeed?

Then again, there are some people who never in a century of Sundays can hide their underlying confusion and caution. They subscribe to *Gourmet* and its satellites, and even submit incredibly complicated recipes to the subeditors, which are discreetly rearranged before publication in some such dutiful department as "Letters to Our Chef." They belong to local food-and-wine groups or their reasonable facsimiles, and bring back packages of musty filé powder from New Orleans, and order snails (packed as a special inducement with the shells wrapped separately) from a former maître d'hôtel who lives next to the airport in Lisbon. They have Grossman's *Guide* on their shelves, and Saintsbury and Schoonmaker, and they serve the proper wines at the proper times and temperatures. They know Escoffier's basic sauces. Their dinners march formally from start to finish.

And over everything, over all the thought and the earnest planning, lies a weight of uncomfortable caution. It is invisible of course and cannot even be identified except by the gastronomically wary, but it shows with damning clearness in the polite faces of the guests, in the genteelly labored tempo of the conversation, and in the well-bred avoidance of any direct mention of the pleasures of the table.

The guests eat well, drink like kings, and go their separate ways unsatisfied. The tired host lies puzzled on his bed, unable to tell himself why he has had no fun, no fun at all, in spite of the thought and effort that went into his little celebration. Why do other people give such amusing dinner parties, he wonders. I tried and *tried*, and did *just* what they all do. . . .

That is the thing: the cautious host's need to follow, to rely on other people's plans. That is what spreads such faint but inescapable vapors of timidity and insecurity over his fine plates and glasses and whatever lies upon and in them. He does not trust himself—more often than not with some justification.

The art of dining has settled upon a basically sound pattern in the last hundred years or less, so that in an instinctive progression of textures and flavors a good classical meal goes from hors d'oeuvres through soup and fish and meat and cheese to the final "sweet conceits" of some dessert designed to amuse rather than excite appetites already more than satisfied. Anyone who wishes may follow this traditional pattern, and his success will be the greater if he is willing to admit, as do present-day princes of gastronomy, that he may occasionally slip into a heretical habit which must be corrected. (A delightful example of this was the decision, made in Paris late in 1947 at the Third International Congress of Gastronomy, that pâté de foie gras must henceforth be served in its proper place at the beginning of a meal, and not later with the salad as has increasingly become the custom!) It shows no caution, no lack of self-assurance, to lean on this classical schedule, for it is the most natural one in modern Western living.

Damning timidity, which can dampen any fine gastronomical fires at table, springs, I suppose, from the fact that the cautious host is incapable of enjoying himself. I know one nationally famous "gourmet" who has absolutely no innate good taste, whose meals are incredibly and coarsely and vulgarly overelaborate and rich, but who presents them with such contagious high spirits that they are unfailingly delightful.

I also know at least four people who have plenty of money for the more Lucullan tidbits of cookery, as well as a devouring desire to be good hosts, whose banquets are dreaded and, more often than not, bluntly shunned. I sit through them now and then because I admire their dogged earnestness. I always wish desperately, compassionately, that my hosts could summon enough gastronomical courage to turn their backs on rote and plan a meal dictated by no matter what faint glimmer of appetite within them rather than by other men's rules.

A supper of two or three ample and savorous courses, with two honest wines to be honestly enjoyed, would do more to kill caution in a good host's soul than all the elaborate menus indelibly engraved in gourmets' history books because of their extravagance and preciosity. I have never met anyone who dined with George Saintsbury, but I am confident that one of his meals could be duplicated, except for the years of the wines, by almost any eager would-be gourmet with enough money, and that it would be a ghastly ordeal for everyone concerned if it were not carried out with the good Professor's zest, his joy of living and eating and drinking and talking in good company.

Here is a dinner served by him in Edinburgh at the end of the last century. It has at worst a horrid fascination to the modern and emasculated palate, but could be, and assuredly was, enjoyable, because the host was not a cautious man:

> Clear soup and then fillets of whiting with a sherry (Dos Cortados, 1873); calf's head à la Terrapin[1] and then oysters en caisses with Château La Frette, 1865; then in proper succession an aspic of tunny, braised beef, roast Guinea fowl, apricots in jelly, velvet cream, anchovies Zadioff,[2] and ices, accompanied by Champagne Giesler 1889, Château Margaux 1870, a La Tache Burgundy of 1886, and an 1870 Port.

This menu is impossible except in its correct classical pattern, and impossible except purely in theory to almost any of today's gastronomical children. But it has a kind of dashing enthusiasm about it. It was not a cautious dinner! It was fun!

I

I cannot find a recipe for this. But perhaps Saintsbury's Terrapin is a cautious Scotch equivalent of à la Tortue.

From what I know of terrapin, most of it vicarious, I would say that Escoffier's Tortue garnish, which includes eggs fried almost without benefit of their whites, comes close to it. The rest of the recipe is interesting in a completely un-Scotch and extravagant way, and it hints at the pains a chef will go to in order to coax his diners to eat a boiled calf's head!

In the Tortue sauce are small quenelles of veal forcemeat with butter, cock's combs and kidneys, pitted stuffed poached olives, slices of truffle, and gherkins cut to the shape of olives. Separate from the "sauced" garnishes are slices of tongue and calf's brain, small trussed poached crayfish, little croutons fried in butter, and the trimmed near-whiteless fried hens' eggs!

To my mind the best recipe for this fantastic hodgepodge of flavors which Professor Saintsbury *may* have served to his guests is the one from Francatelli's *The Modern Cook*, published in London in 1846. It is a tribute to Victorian staunchness.

Calf's Head à la Tortue

Bone, blanch, and trim a calf's head, cut it up into large scollops, keep the ears whole, neatly trim the pieces, and toss them in the juice of a lemon; put them in a stewpan, with carrot, onion, celery, garnished-faggot, cloves, mace, and a few pepper-corns; moisten with half a bottle of Madeira or sherry, and two large ladlefuls of good stock; cover with a well-buttered stiff paper, and put on the lid; set the whole to braize on the stove for about two hours. When the pieces of calf's head are done, drain them on a napkin, and afterwards dish them up, in the form of a close wreath, round the base of a fried bread croustade; place the ears at the ends and on the flanks: if the party be large, two extra ears should be procured, as the four make the dish look much handsomer: next, place the tongue, cut down its centre, and spread out on top of the croustade; on this put the brains, which must be kept whole and white, and round these, on the croustade, should be stuck six ornamental silver skewers, garnished with a double cocks-comb, a large mushroom, a quenelle, a truffle, and a large crayfish; sauce around with a well made sauce à la

Tortue; garnish the dish round between the spaces of the ears with four larded and glazed sweetbreads, and eight decorated quenelles, *and send to table.*

2

I have searched through several cookbooks which might have been used by Professor Saintsbury, and I am defeated: no oysters en caisses, no savory called anything even approximating anchovies Zadioff. Perhaps they were staring at me, and I was too dazed by all the other Victorian dishes to see them.

But I can remember once in England, in a fairly Victorian household and in spite of the year (1936 or so), being served, at the end of a dinner which began with plovers' eggs, a kind of cold appetizer-tickler, rather a change from the usual hot over-spicy British fillip to a good meal. They were little coffins, as Elizabethan manuals would have named them, of rich pastry, generously filled with black caviar and with one trimmed handsome oyster resting upon each dark bed. What a strange and intrinsically stimulating flavor at the end of the rococo menu!

D *is for*
Dining *out*

. . . and its amenities.

A great deal has been written about the amenities of dining, but few writers have seen fit to comment on the very important modern problem of eating in a public place.

I had a happy beginning in this neglected art and much abused privilege, one that has sheathed it in unfading pleasure for me when it is done well. When I was no more than five or so my father and mother would begin to prepare my spirits for Easter, or Christmas, or a birthday, and when the festival rolled around, there I would be, waiting to greet it in my wide hat with ribbons, on the pink velvet seat of the region's best restaurant.

At first it was called Marcel's, I believe. By now Hollywood and its New York refugees have widened the choice if not the choiceness, and there are several eating houses within a hundred miles of me in which I am delighted to be seen. I have friends who feel the same way. The problem, given that situation, is how most smoothly to combine our presences at the same public table.

I admit that I am prejudiced about it. I seldom dine out, and because of my early conditioning to the sweet illusion of permanent celebration, of "party" and festivity on every such occasion, I feel automatically that any invitation means sure excitement, that it will be an event, whether it brings me a rained-on hamburger[1] in a drive-in or Chicken Jerusalem at Perino's. The trouble is, I am afraid, that I expect the people I dine with to feel the same muted but omnipresent delight that I feel.

They seldom do. More often than not they eat out (and what a dreadfully glum phrase that is!) several times each week. They have business lunches: in a small town, service clubs and Chamber of Commerce meetings and so on; in a city, conferences with colleagues they must quickly dominate. In both cases, no matter what type of food is served, they are tense, wary, and gastronomically bored to the point of coma. As for their dinners, those too are at best a frank mixture of business and pleasure. The attitude seems to be that all humans must eat, and all humans must make money in order to eat, and therefore the two things might as well be combined.

The result of this is a common sight in any restaurant from the Black Kat on South Main to Mike Romanoff's on Rodeo Drive: carefully dressed women are very polite to other carefully dressed women while their male companions walk in invisible circles around one another, sniffing out the chances of anything from laying a new plastic tile floor in the bathroom to trading top stars for two hundred grand.

Such luncheons and dinners are the reason, fairly obviously, that successful people have gastric ulcers. I, on the other hand, may be less successful, but I have never been menaced by that dreadful burning sensation, which is laughingly called occupational but is more likely to be known in the future as merely twentieth-century. I refuse, almost categorically, to dine out. I refuse to have my childhood dreams of fun and excitement turned into a routine and ungracious feeding, to the tune of wifely chitchat and the clink of unmade dollars.

However, there are occasions on which one must do so, and one of these was the time I took a Very Important Person to dinner. He had often entertained me and various glamorous groups with lavish simplicity in his home, with its electrically shaken cocktails, electrically lighted swimming pool, and electrically rotated spit. I thought it would be a compliment to him to cook dinner for him myself, as soon as I got a place to cook it in. But no: I was tipped off with elaborate tact by his wife, his secretary, and the secretary of his immediate superior in the studio, that he felt bad, in fact terrible, that I had not "entertained" him. All right, I said, all right; forgetting my disappointment in a deliberate campaign to do the thing as nearly as possible as I thought it should be done in a public eating place.

I telephoned the restaurant the day before and asked for a table in accord with my friend's local importance. This obviated standing in line, which is ignominious no matter how diplomatically the line may be spread through the bar by a good headwaiter.

Then I ordered the meal, to be served to four people. It was dictated by what I could remember of my honored guest's tastes, just as it would have been in my home. He boasted of being a meat-and-potato boy, a hater of fancy sauces, a lover of Scotch in moderation, and a shunner of any but chilled pink wine. Very well: smoked salmon, a small rack of lamb, potatoes Anna, Belgian endive salad, and a tray of Langlois Blue, Rouge et Noir Camembert, Wisconsin Swiss, and Teleme Jack cheese; Scotch or sherry first, and then Louis Martini's Gamay Rosé. It was not my idea of a perfect meal, but it could be eaten with no pain.

By ordering in advance I avoided another horrible barrier to decent dining out: the confusion that inevitably follows the first showing of menu cards to more than two people at once.

The waiter waits. The diners ponder, stutter, variously flaunting their ignorance or their pretensions to knowledge. They mutter and murmur into the air, assuming Godlike clarity of hearing on the part of the poor harried servant and disregarding entirely the fact that they are guests at a table. The men usually blurt some stock familiar order. Women hum, sip their cocktails, and change their minds at least twice after the waiter has scrawled on his pad. There is a general feeling of chaos, and nobody seems to realize that if the same human beings were invited to any normal home they would not dream of giving their orders so confusedly and arbitrarily, nor would the hostess dare leave her guests thus tenderly exposed. No, a good meal inside or outside the private circle should be ordered in advance (or at least ordered with great firmness by the host at table in a restaurant), to avoid this distressing welter of words and the resultant unrelated odors, plates, servings, when a group has gone helter-skelter through a menu.

The third thing I did was to see the headwaiter and tip him. And since I knew the restaurant and the good relations therein between the various professional levels, I left another tip with him for the man who would take care of us come eight o'clock.

The final step: I arranged for the bill to be mailed to me. There are few things more boringly painful about public dining, to my mind, than the obligatory plunging and grabbing and arguing that are taken as a matter of course at the end of a meal. If men are present they look on it as an insult to their virility to let a woman pay. If women are eating together, they simply outshriek one another, and the noisiest bears off the check in expensive but curiously rewarding triumph. I feel rebuffed, when I have invited anyone of no matter what sex to dine with me, to have the bill snatched gallantly from me, just as I would feel in-sulted if after dining in my home a guest slipped a bill under his plate for the groceries I had used.

When I walked out of the restaurant I felt that I had done everything I could to assure my friend of a meal which I could have given him for one-fourth the cost and about one-eighth the bother at home, but which he would, because of his peculiar importance in a very peculiar industry, enjoy a hundred times as much because it was in this peculiar town's smartest eating place.

Everything went beautifully. The table was the "right" one socially, the Scotch was from the proper dimpled bottle, the waiter scudded on velvet, other Very Important People nodded and smiled. The slices of salmon were *so* thin, and the wine came and the rack of lamb, a masterpiece, the headwaiter cool as a surgeon above it.

My guest turned to me, for the first of many times that night, and said, "Do you know, in my whole life nobody has ever ordered a meal just for me?"

"Nonsense," I said, thinking of all the dinners that people had served him, people who for one reason or another wanted to please him—as I did.

"No," he said—by the end of the evening tearfully—"no, never! And I hate menus. I hate them. I go to places where they know what I want just so I don't have to look at menus. If I pretend to look, I have something memorized to say. If my doctor has told me to eat tomatoes I say, 'A fresh tomato omelet'—something like that to make them pay a little attention to me. Now and then I get peeved at all the French and I say, '*Spécialité de la maison*'—how's my accent? But, do you know, this is the first time anyone ever realized that I hate menus and having to order and—do you know, this is just like a party!"

It would be easy here for me to indicate that at this somewhat maudlin point my guest slid under the table. He did not. It was a good evening, with good talk, even in Hollywood where the fact that we were enjoying ourselves in public proved us embarrassingly out of line. It had about it something, no matter how faint, of the festive ease, the latent excitement, of my childhood celebrations—a reward to me for having observed the basic principles of decent dining out. I had treated my guest as much as possible as if he were in my home, and "miracles occurred."

I

A recipe which was whispered awesomely to me as being the authentic one used by a famous restaurant was a strange, sloppy mixture of ground sirloin, raw egg, salt and pepper and mustard, Worcestershire sauce, and an impossible quantity of rich chicken broth. Perhaps it is authentic. Perhaps if this quasi-soup is mixed and allowed to stand, it will thicken itself enough to be made into cakes fit to broil. Cynically I say no.

It is easy to make very good hamburgers, given the same ingredients in more realistic proportions, and given, of course, the acceptance of the modern American meaning of hamburger: chopped meat formed into cakes, cooked, and served on or in a split bun.

When I was much younger and proportionately hungrier and less finicky, a minor form of bliss was going to a drive-in near school and eating two or three weird, adulterated combinations of fried beef, mayonnaise, tomato catsup, shredded lettuce, melted cheese, unidentifiable relish, and sliced onion. These concoctions were called "Rite-Spot Specials," in dubious honor of the place that served them. They seemed wonderful then. Now I gag.

Now I prepare, from time to time, an austere and fine adaptation of this adolescent dream. It is as much better than the old as being my age is than being that age—and that is a lot! Served with some sourdough bread, a bowl of fresh celery or plain green salad, and some simple red wine or beer, it is good.

Hamburgers
(à la Mode de Moi-même)

1½ to 2 lbs. best sirloin, trimmed of fat and coarsely ground (or finely chopped)	1 cup mixed chopped onion, parsley, green pepper, herbs, each according to taste
1 cup ordinary red table wine	4 tablespoons oyster sauce (Chinese or American) or 2 tablespoons Worcestershire sauce
3 or 4 tablespoons butter	

Shape meat firmly into four round patties at least 1½ inches thick. Have the skillet very hot. Sear the meat (very smoky procedure) on both sides and remove at once to a hot buttered platter, where the meat will continue to heat through. (Extend the searing time if rare meat is not wanted.)

Remove the skillet from the fire. When slightly cooled, put the wine and butter in it and swirl, to collect what Brillat-Savarin would have called the "osmazome." Return to heat and toss in the chopped ingredients, and cover closely. Turn off heat as soon as these begin to hiss. Remove from stove, take off cover, add oyster sauce, swirl once more, and pour over hot meat. Serve at once, since the heat contained in the sauce and the patties continues the cooking process.

E *is for* Exquisite

. . . and its gastronomical connotations, at least for me.

When I hear of a gourmet with exquisite taste I assume, perhaps too hastily and perhaps very wrongly, that there is something exaggeratedly elaborate, and even languidly perverted, about his gourmandism. I do not think simply of an exquisitely laid table and an exquisite meal. Instead I see his silver carved in subtly erotic patterns, and his courses following one upon another in a cabalistic design, half pain, half pleasure. I take it for granted, in spite of my good sense, that rare volumes on witchcraft have equal place with Escoffier in his kitchen library, and I read into his basic recipe for meat stock a dozen deviously significant ingredients.

Such deliberate romanticism on my part can most easily be dismissed as the wishful thinking of an amateur cook who scrambles eggs very well but only reads, these days, about filets de sole Polignac and pâté de foie truffé en brioche. Or perhaps it is Freudian: subconsciously I might murder, or even seduce, by means of cookery, and therefore I ascribe such potentialities to someone whose culinary freedom I envy! Whatever the reason, in my private lexicon of gastronomy I continue to see the word exquisite ringed about with subtle vapors of perversion.

Most of the great historical and literary gourmets, in the sense of their being exquisites, have had the unlimited money, like Des Esseintes in Huysmans' *Against the Grain*. The very fact that they can command no matter what incredible delicacy adds to their satiety, and that in turn gives just the fillip of distortion to their appetites which satisfies my definition of their exquisiteness.

Huysmans' sad young man, for instance: his "farewell dinner to a temporarily dead virility," as the invitations shaped like bereavement notices called it, was a masterpiece of jaded extravagance. He needed to be a millionaire, as well as a determined exquisite, to serve—in a black-draped room lighted by green flames, attended by nude black virgins wearing silver slippers and stockings trimmed with dripping tears—a dinner beginning with blackest caviar and ending with black-heart cherries. He needed to be at least a demi-millionaire to fill his fountain with ink for that one dubious feast, and to line his ash-covered paths with funereal pine trees.

He needed, above all, to be sublimely indifferent to the taint of vulgarity, for his earnest efforts at eccentricity were indeed vulgar, and ridiculous too, in a basically shameful and extravagant way. All that saved him from oblivion was his dignified disregard of anything but his own kind of pleasure.

It is the same with some of the dishes we still read about with a strange fascination, those cooked for the most dissipated of the Romans two thousand years or so ago. Doubtless many of them tried to astound their sycophants by serving whole platters of the tongues of little birds that had been trained to talk before they went into the pot. We do not remember the names of these men, nor anything more than the vulgarly idiotic waste. But what if one of those epicures, greatly in love with a proud lady named Livia, had taught a thousand birds to sing her name, Livia, Livia, to the moment of most perfect diction, and then had served forth to the lady a fine pie of their tongues, split, honeyed, and impaled on twigs of myrrh? *Then*, I think, that fat lover would still be known to us for what he was, an exquisite— a silly one perhaps, extravagant certainly, but with his own dignity about him.

I remember deciding once, long ago and I believe after reading Elwanger's *Pleasures of the Table* for the first time, that the most exquisite dish I had ever heard of was a salad of satiny white endive with large heavily scented Parma violets scattered through it. It meant everything subtle and intense and aesthetically significant in my private gastronomy, just as, a few years earlier, a brown-skinned lover with a turquoise set in one ear lobe epitomized my adolescent dream of passion. It is a misfortune perhaps that not many months ago the salad¹ was set before me in a bowl.

That it was not very good was relatively unimportant: the dressing was light to the point of being innocuous, and it was unable to stand up under the perfumed assault of the blossoms. What disappointed me, finally and forever, was that it was served neither exquisitely, nor by an exquisite, nor with an exquisite disregard of the vulgar.

Instead it was concocted and presented with both affectation and awkwardness and was at best an attempt at that insidious decadence which is a prerequisite of my definition. It suddenly became ridiculous.

I blushed for my long dream of it and felt a hollowness, for where again will I know so certainly that such and such a dish is *it*? What will it be? Expense is not enough, for sure, and no intricate silverware, no ritual of serving and compounding, can guarantee the magic. There must, for me at least, be a faint nebular madness, dignified no matter how deliberate, to a dinner that is exquisite.

I

Eastern Americans find it an all-too-easy gastronomical gambit to sneer, no matter how genteelly, at the Western habit of serving a salad before a main, or meat, course at dinner.

I used to do this in a kind of reverse snobbism. I learned in Northern California why I was wrong.

There people know how to drink table wine better than anywhere else in the United States, and there they are much influenced by fellow countrymen of French and Italian descent who would never cut into a good wine's attack on human taste buds by adding vinegar or lemon juice or even mustard to the battle.

There they are not afraid to lead up to the triumph of a heady entrée and its accompanying bottle by such sturdily subtle flavors as a fresh tomato can give, or garden lettuce touched with a garlic bud, or a morsel of anchovy. In Napa or Livermore or Sonoma a roadside boarding-house will serve such an antipasto as would please any finicky gourmet strong enough to meet the wine he wanted.

There an approximation of the classical tossed green salad may well be part of any laborer's daily fare, as a prelude to the meat and the wine that must mainly nourish him, and not as a routine sourish aftermath, tackled without appetite or interest simply because it has become traditional elsewhere to serve the salad after the roast.

The nearest I ever came to the fresh, crude before-meat salads of Northern California was in Venice, in 1940, when an extraordinarily keen porter at the hotel found us a gondolier who was possessed of the gourmet's "curious nose" if ever I did hear of it.

Vittorio, whom we hired by the week, paddled us dreamily from one *trattoria* to another, and we would jump bobbily from the gondola into its dappled garden-restaurant and then two or three hours later sag carefully back again into our little ship, full of a number of good things, none of which I can remember except the omnipresent scampi, the little shrimps of foul repute which Casanova's mother cried out for the night before his birth, and the salads. (The coffee was fine too.)

The salads stood in common white kitchen bowls and platters for the most part, in two or three linen-covered tiers upon a table at one side of the garden. Every vegetable had an immediate life to it, so that the tiny potatoes boiled in their skins *almost* crunched, but not enough to repel; the dozen different kinds of artichokes were *almost* tough; the celery poached in chicken broth *almost* felt raw between the teeth. It was somewhat like Chinese food, fresh but purified, and my husband remarked casually that this, as well as the untoward delicacy and flavor of everything, was probably because of the Venetian night soil it was grown in. I continued to delight in it, and to point like a happy child at this bowl, that platter, and then watch my waiter toss the little morsels together in a salad that may be well known to every traveler but me. It served as a fine introduction to whatever followed rather than as a dutiful tonic afterward.

I continue to find many people, especially Englishmen and Americans, who because of their early gastronomical education (or lack of it) cannot enjoy a fresh salad before the entrée. Then I serve it after the entrée, but I try to suit the seasoning to what has gone before and make it bland in proportion to the wine being drunk. One thing I do not do is use lemon juice when we are drinking anything good—which to my mind is any honest wine ever bottled, of no matter what year or price. I use a good wine vinegar: I do not hold much with the fancy bottled tarragon vinegars and such, although herb vinegars have their own place in seasoning. Sometimes I cheat, silently of course, and use no vinegar at all, but an extra dash of soy, or of oyster sauce after lamb, for instance.

I almost never serve such fundamentally sharp things as tomatoes in a salad after meat, feeling that they, like vinegar, cut into the wonderful action of wine upon the tongue. Now and then I put in a pinch of good curry powder, or fresh minced anise, to baffle people. (I have yet to try hard enough to astonish them by using Paul Reboux's trick of tiny matchsticks of carrot and an equal quantity of tiny matchsticks of orange peel, which are of identical color but such different tastes!)

Mostly I depend on oil, the best I can buy. I like a heavy, greenish, very strong olive oil, from California or Spain. I do not like the highly refined oils I have been served, with such elation, from Italy: my palate is probably too crude for them. A few times in France I have eaten salad made with the now rare walnut oil . . . delicious! I truly dislike American vegetable oils, but on the other hand I grew to enjoy the huile d'arachides, rather like our kosher peanut oil, which I used in Dijon and Switzerland between wars.

Now and then I like to put tomatoes, sliced onions (preferably those pretty rose-blue ones), garden greens, fresh chopped herbs, some anchovy fillets or a boiled sliced potato or a hard-cooked egg, into a bowl, sprinkle them with salt, freshly ground pepper, vinegar, and oil, and toss them around lightly, the Italian way, the way hungry Venetian waiters on their days off from the big restaurants in San Francisco do it for themselves at places like La Tosca, while the jukeboxes throb "Return to Sorrento" and "Now Is the Hour."

Occasionally I read, with sick fascination, the ads for elaborate household gadgets in the slick-paper magazines. The last one I saw said, in ten varying types to astound me, "The New Salad-master! Make salads you will be proud of! This new all-purpose, marvelous, revolutionary, indispensable kitchen aid will make *you* a cook! It chops, peels, waffles, grates, strings, shreds, crimps, cuts, and slices lettuce in a second! Free wonderful salad recipes!"

Could the people in Venice have been wrong with those forthright bowls of little whole poached potatoes, scalded whole beans as thick as a needle, whole peas fragrant as flowers?

F *is for*
Family

. . . and the depths and heights of gastronomical enjoyment to be found at the family board.

It is possible, indeed almost too easy, to be eloquently sentimental about large groups of assorted relatives who gather for Christmas or Thanksgiving or some such festival, and eat and drink and gossip and laugh together. They always laugh: in Norman Rockwell magazine covers and in Iowa novels and in any currently popular variation of "I Remember Mustache Cups" there is Gargantuan laughter, from toothless babe to equally toothless Gramp. Great quantities of home-cooked goodies are consumed, great pitchers of Uncle Nub's hard cider are quaffed, and great gusts of earthy merriment sweep like prairie fire around the cluttered table. The men folk bring out their whittling knives in postprandial digestive calm, the women (sometimes spelled *wimmin* to denote an inaudible provincialism) chatter and scrape and swab down in the kitchen, and the bulging children *bulge*.

The cold truth is that family dinners are more often than not an ordeal of nervous indigestion, preceded by hidden resentment and ennui and accompanied by psychosomatic jitters.

The best way to guarantee smooth sailing at one of them is to assemble the relatives only when a will must be read. This at least presupposes good manners during the meal, if the lawyer is not scheduled to appear until after it. Funeral baked meats have perhaps been more enjoyed than any christening cakes or wedding pottages, thanks largely to the spice of wishful thinking that subtly flavors them, as yet untouched by disappointment, dread, or hatred.

My own experience with family dinners has fallen somewhere between this facile irony and the bucolic lustiness of popular idealization. I remember that several times at Christmas there were perhaps twenty of us at the Ranch for a lengthy noon dinner, to which none of us was accustomed. I always had fun, being young and healthy and amenable, but I do not recall, perhaps to my shame, that I had any *special* fun.

To be truthful, I was conscious by my eleventh or twelfth year that there was about the whole ceremony a kind of doggedness, a feeling that in spite of hell and high water we were duty-bound to go through with it, because my grandfather was very old and might not live another year, or because a cousin had just lost her abominable but very rich husband, or because another cousin was going to Stanford instead of Yale at Yale's request and so would be with us, or something like that. It was tacitly understood that the next day would find my sister Anne droopy and bilious, my mother overtired, and the cook crankily polishing glasses and eying the piles of the "best" Irish linen that had to be laundered. My father, on the other hand, would still be glowing: he loved any kind of party in the world, even a family one.

I seem, and I am thankful for it, to have inherited some of his capacity for enjoying such intramural sport, combined, fortunately, with my mother's ability to cope with it. In spite of my conviction that a group of deliberately assembled relatives can be one of the dullest, if not most dangerous, gatherings in the world, I am smugly foolhardy enough to have invited all my available family, more than once, to dine with me.

The last time was perhaps the most daring, and it went off with a dash and smoothness that will always bulwark my self-esteem, for it was the happy result of many days of thought and preparation.

Parents, cousins, new generation—all came. It meant hotel reservations in the near-by town, and great supplies of food and drink for a long holiday during which the stores were closed. It meant wood stored under cover for the fireplace in case of rain (it poured), and Band-Aids and liniment (my nephew and my two-year-old daughter fell off a boulder into the pond), and considerable self-control (my favorite male shot several of my favorite quail).

It meant a lot of work: I was cook, and before the festival I had food prepared or at least in line for an average of twelve persons a meal, three meals a day, for three days. And the right good wines. And the other potables, right, good, and copious. That, I say smugly, is no mean feat.

It was exciting and rewarding and completely deliberate. Nothing, to my knowledge at least, went wrong. There was an aura of gaiety and affection all about us—and that too, with people of different ages and sexes and beliefs, political and religious *and* social, is also something of a feat to attain and to maintain. The whole thing, for a miracle to bless me, went off well.

This is most often the case in planned celebrations, I think. Now and then there is a happy accident in families, and brothers and cousins and grandparents who may have been cold or even warlike suddenly find themselves in some stuffy booth in a chophouse, eating together with forgotten warmth and amity.

But it is rare. Most often it must be prearranged with care and caution.

It must not simply be taken for granted that a given set of ill-assorted people, for no other reason than because it is Christmas, will be joyful to be reunited and to break bread together. They must be jolted, even shocked, into excitement and surprise and subsequent delight. All the old routine patterns of food and flowers and cups must be redistributed, to break up that mortal ignominy of the family dinner, when what has too often been said and felt and thought is once more said, felt, and thought: slow poison in every mouthful, old grudges, new hateful boredom, nascent antagonism and resentment—why in God's name does Mother always put her arm *that* way on the chair, and why does Helen's girdle always pop as she lifts the denuded meat platter up and away from Father, and why does Sis always tap her fingers thus tinnily against the rim of her wine glass? Poison, indeed, and most deeply to be shunned!

It takes courage to give a family party, and at least once I had enough to do it, being mightier in my youth than I am now. I was almost stony broke, unable to take no matter how judicious a collection of relatives to a decent restaurant. So . . .

I summoned my father, mother, brother, and sisters to a supper in the Ranch dining-room, to celebrate nothing at all. I managed to pay for it, almost to the least grain of salt: silly, but a sop to my proud young soul. I set the table with the family's best silver and china and crystal (especially the iridescent and incredibly thin wine goblets we have always had for "party").

I went to Bernstein's on the Park in Los Angeles and bought beautiful fresh shellfish: tiny bay shrimp in their shells, crab cooked while I waited, and lobster claws too, pink prawns, little mussels in their purple shells. I went down behind the Plaza and bought flat round loaves of sourdough bread and good spaghetti and sweet butter. I bought some real cheese, not the kind that is made of by-products and melted into tinfoil blocks. I bought Wente Brothers' Grey Riesling and Italian-Swiss Colony Tipo Red, and some over-roasted coffee blended on Piuma's drugstore counter for me. There, in short, was the skeleton of the feast.

The flesh upon this bony structure was a more artful thing, compounded of my prejudices and my enthusiastic beliefs. It is true that my comparative youngness made me more eager to do battle than I would be now, but I still think I was right to rebel against some of the inevitable boredom of dining *en famille*.

To begin with, I reseated everyone. I was tired of seeing my father looming against the massive ugliness of the sideboard, with that damned square mirror always a little crooked behind his right ear. I assumed, somewhat grandly, that he was equally tired of looking down the table toward my mother, forever masked behind a collection of cigarette boxes, ash trays, sugar shakers left there whether needed or not, a Louis Quinze snuff box full of saccharin, several salt shakers, a battered wooden pepper mill, and an eternal bouquet, fresh but uninspired, of whatever could be gleaned from the garden. With never a yea or nay to guide me I eliminated this clutter from the center of the table—it had been on my nerves for at least fifteen years—and in a low bowl I arranged "bought" camellias instead of a "grown" bunch of this-or-that from the side yard.

My parents were rocked on their bases, to put it mildly, and only innate good manners kept them from shying away from my crazy plan like startled and resentful deer whose drinking place has been transferred.

Those were my first and most drastic attempts, clumsy enough, I admit, but very successful in the end, to break up what seemed to me a deadly dull pattern. Then I used the sideboard as a buffet, which had never been done before in our memory. I tipped off my siblings beforehand, and we forced my father to get up and get his own first course of shellfish, which he enjoyed enormously after he recovered from the first shock of not having someone wait on him. He poked and sniffed and puttered happily over the beautiful platters of shrimp and suchlike and made a fine plate of things for my mother, who sat with an almost shy smile, letting the newness of this flood gently, unforgettably, into her sensitive mind and heart.

My brother poured the cold Grey Riesling with a flourish, assuming what had always been Father's prerogative. Later I served the casserole of spaghetti, without its eternal family accompaniment of rich sauce, and it was doubly delicious for that flouting of tradition.'

The Tipo was good. The Tipo flowed. So, happy magic, did our talk. There we were, solidly one for those moments at least, leaning our arms easily along the cool wood, reaching without thought for our little cups of hot bitter coffee or our glasses, not laughing perhaps as the families do in the pictures and the stories, but with our eyes loving and deep, one to another. It was good, worth the planning. It made the other necessary mass meals more endurable, more a part of being that undeniable rock, the Family.

I

There is an inevitable ritual about serving and eating spaghetti. Sometimes when I have endured the pompous stewings and simmerings and scrapings and tastings of an amateur chef's performance (for it can be called no less), I have felt that nothing at all would be preferable. But, fortunately for me, I like good spaghetti too well to forego it.

The first time I ever saw it eaten as it should be, in varying degrees of longness and a fine uniformity of writhing limpness and buttery richness and accompanying noisy sounds, I was fairly young, fourteen or so. I was old enough to be conscious of wearing my best manners, for I was upstairs in Los Angeles' one elegant restaurant, and the fact that it was Ignace Paderewski I watched with such fascination did nothing to alleviate my priggish horror at the spectacle. That he was obviously enjoying himself could not, at my tender age, mean much: I still thought in terms of being sent away from the table for glupping and spilling, both of which he did nonchalantly. For a long time I pondered on the whole strange sight.

What undoubtedly made it stranger still to me was the way spaghetti was always served at home. There it was, and still is, the cook's easiest choice for using leftover beef or lamb. In spite of the mediocrity of inspiration, we loved its soft texture and its warmth, the little broken lengths of pasta, the various bits of meat crumbs and tomato and cheese, and the crust that formed on top of it in the baking. We still do, and no matter what life has done to our taste buds, when we are home for a week end or a week, we hope there will be enough fried chicken or pot roast left for Helen to make spaghetti.

My natural revolt against this uninspired, misbegotten pattern filled me, when I left the nest, with overenthusiasm for the gymnastics of the amateurs, and I hate now to think of the sticky lukewarm messes I have happily downed, sitting, ah, *vie bohème*, upon a dirty studio floor with a glass of red ink beside me. But, come to think of it, I do *not* hate that thought! I look back on it, relieved both to be able to look back and to have its unthinking youthful liveliness to look back *on*.

I prefer, I add with no haste, the present. I prefer, infinitely, my own routine for making and serving spaghetti, for I have come to admit that no matter how simply it is done, it involves enough calculation and timing to qualify as a real performance, like any theatrical routine. There is an apt description of it, by James M. Cain, in Merle Armitage's *Fit for a King*. What he says about the quickness and the hotness of everything is what I too would say. He gives typically virile recipes for two sauces to be served with the plain cooked spaghetti, according to taste. Then he writes, "There is always one peculiar fellow, the same one who always puts salt in his beer, who likes his with butter only, so a little butter on the table won't hurt."

Now I never put salt in my beer, nor do I ever plan to. But I am one of Mr. Cain's "peculiar fellows" in that I like not only spaghetti but every other form of pastasciutta without a trace of the popular and indeed socially requisite sauces that always coat them or swim alongside. I go so far as never to serve them at my own table, and I can add smugly that many a confirmed sauce-man has left my table converted to my theory that nothing helps fresh hot spaghetti as much as a plenitude of sweet butter, freshly ground pepper, and good grated Parmesan cheese, all added at top speed and tossed and mixed regardless of fourteen-year-old stares like the one I gave the innocent Paderewski, the whole washed down with a good Chianti or a Tipo Red.

I must confess that it is in a way harder to achieve my seeming simplicity, hew to my chastity of design, than to ask some one of my eager food-and-wine club acquaintances to come in and devastate the kitchen in the creation of one of his Famous Spaghetti Dinners. I can remember all too many weighty pinches of saffron and thunderous hints of sweet marjoram, in the name of this gastronomical oddity, and cannot help feeling, in all cynicism, that a quantity of preprandial highballs had more to do with the half-famished guests' acclamations than did any real goodness in the dish itself.

I have watched a great many off-the-record culinary shows, nonprofessional of course, and I think that the production of a large platter of spaghetti in its sauce calls forth more of the prima donna in the average amateur cook than anything, except, perhaps, crêpes Suzette. One otherwise sober friend of mine goes so far as to assemble all the guests, let them watch a few simple but dramatic processes such as searing the chopped beef and then dousing the blue-black choking fumes with red wine, and immediately afterward makes his invited spectators leave the kitchen, at once, peremptorily, and bound to silence, while he bends tensely over a secret packet of spices he has procured at great expense and brought, seemingly, to the noisy staccato of gunfire from rival chefs who would kill him for his treasure and the proportions therein.

Here is the way, ridiculous anticlimax, that I myself serve spaghetti and prefer that it be served to me. I am, to quote Mr. Cain again, "peculiar."

Have a bowl of grated Parmesan, genuine and sandy and unadulterated by domestic packaged stuff; a large pat of sweet butter; a good salt shaker and a freshly filled pepper mill; as many hot plates as there are people, and a big, hot casserole with a lump of butter melting in the bottom.

Cook good spaghetti rapidly in plenty of boiling water. (If the spaghetti is really reputable I do not salt the pot.) When half cooked add a lump of butter or a tablespoonful of olive oil; this keeps the water from boiling over and seems to eliminate the danger of sticking. When a strand of the spaghetti (of course not broken beforehand) can be pinched between my thumb and forefinger, I think it is done, somewhat more than *al dente* but not too soft. Then pour it, throw it almost, into a big colander, dash very cold water thoroughly through it and then boiling hot water even more thoroughly (I know this is a heinous procedure to some gastronomical purists), and shake it furiously to dry it off a little. Pour it, blazing hot, into the almost sizzling casserole, and serve it immediately on the equally hot plate of whoever is hungry for it.

The next step precludes any so-called table manners: it must be carried out with rapidity, a skill easy to enlarge by pleasurable practice, and undaunted enthusiasm. Put a generous lump of sweet butter on top of the pile of spaghetti (first served first come . . .); shake and twist on the salt and pepper, also generously; pile Parmesan on top, and with your fork mix the whole into an odorous, steamy, rich, Medusa-like tangle.

All that is left is to eat it. That, according to the general air of *bien-être* and relaxation which should by now have spread through the company, is perhaps best left undescribed. Let us say that Paderewski did it beautifully.

G *is for*
Gluttony

. . . and why and how it is that.

It is a curious fact that no man likes to call himself a glutton, and yet each of us has in him a trace of gluttony, potential or actual. I cannot believe that there exists a single coherent human being who will not confess, at least to himself, that once or twice he has stuffed himself to the bursting point, on anything from quail financière[1] to flapjacks, for no other reason than the beastlike satisfaction of his belly. In fact I pity anyone who has not permitted himself this sensual experience, if only to determine what his own private limitations are, and where, for himself alone, gourmandism ends and gluttony begins.

It is different for each of us, and the size of a man's paunch has little to do with the kind of appetite which fills it. Diamond Jim Brady, for instance, is more often than not called "the greatest glutton in American history," and so on, simply because he had a really enormous capacity for food. To my mind he was not gluttonous but rather monstrous, in that his stomach was about six times normal size. That he ate at least six times as much as a normal man did not make him a glutton. He was, instead, Gargantuan, in the classical sense. His taste was keen and sure to the time of his death, and that he ate nine portions of sole Marguéry the night George Rector brought the recipe back to New York from Paris especially for him does not mean that he gorged himself on it but simply that he had room for it.

I myself would like to be able to eat that much of something I really delight in, and I can recognize overtones of envy in the way lesser mortals so easily damned Brady as a glutton, even in the days of excess when he flourished.

Probably this country will never again see so many fat, rich men as were prevalent at the end of the last century, copper kings and railroad millionaires and suchlike literally stuffing themselves to death in imitation of Diamond Jim, whose abnormally large stomach coincided so miraculously with the period. He ate a hundred men like "Betcha-Million" Gates into their oversized coffins simply because he was a historical accident, and it is interesting to speculate on what his influence would be today, when most of the robber barons have gastric ulcers and lunch off crackers and milk at their desks. Certainly it is now unfashionable to overeat in public, and the few real trenchermen left are careful to practice their gastronomical excesses in the name of various honorable and respected food-and-wine societies.

It is safe to say, I think, that never again in our civilization will gluttony be condoned, much less socially accepted, as it was at the height of Roman decadence, when a vomitorium was as necessary a part of any well-appointed home as a powder room is today, and throat ticklers were as common as our Kleenex. That was, as one almost forgotten writer has said in an unforgettable phrase, the "period of insatiable voracity and the peacock's plume," and I am glad it is far behind me, for I would make but a weak social figure of a glutton, no matter to what excesses of hunger I could confess.

My capacity is very limited, fortunately for my inward as well as outer economy, so that what gluttonizing I have indulged in has resulted in biliousness more spiritual than physical. It has, like almost everyone's in this century, been largely secret. I think it reached its peak of purely animal satisfaction when I was about seventeen.

I was cloistered then in a school where each avid, yearning young female was allowed to feed at least one of her several kinds of hunger with a daily chocolate bar. I evolved for myself a strangely voluptuous pattern of borrowing, hoarding, begging, and otherwise collecting about seven or eight of these noxious sweets and eating them alone upon a pile of pillows when all the other girls were on the hockey field or some such equally healthful place. If I could eat at the same time a nickel box of soda crackers, brought to me by a stooge among the day girls, my orgiastic pleasure was complete.

I find, in confessing this far-distant sensuality, that even the cool detachment acquired with time does not keep me from feeling both embarrassed and disgusted. What a pig I was!

I am a poor figure of a glutton today in comparison with that frank adolescent cramming. In fact I can think of nothing quite like it in my present make-up. It is true that I overeat at times, through carelessness or a deliberate prolonging of my pleasure in a certain taste, but I do not do it with the voracity of youth. I am probably incapable, really, of such lust. I rather regret it: one more admission of my dwindling powers!

Perhaps the nearest I come to gluttony is with wine. As often as possible, when a really beautiful bottle is before me, I drink all I can of it, even when I know that I have had more than I want physically. That is gluttonous.

But I think to myself, when again will I have this taste upon my tongue? Where else in the world is there just such wine as this, with just this bouquet, at just this heat, in just this crystal cup? And when again will I be alive to it as I am this very minute, sitting here on a green hillside above the sea, or here in this dim, murmuring, richly odorous restaurant, or here in this fisherman's café on the wharf? More, more, I think—all of it, to the last exquisite drop, for there is no satiety for me, nor ever has been, in such drinking.

Perhaps this keeps it from being gluttony—not according to the dictionary but in my own lexicon of taste. I do not know.

I

The word *financière*, for fairly obvious reasons, means richness, extravagance, a nonchalant disregard of the purse, but I sometimes suspect that I use it oftener than it warrants to denote anything Lucullan. I need only reread some Victorian cookery books to reassure myself and justify my preoccupation with the word.

I imagine that now and then, in the remotest dining clubs of London and Lisbon, in the most desperately spendthrift of *nouveaux riches* private kitchens, quails are still served *à la financière*, and unless I am much mistaken they are prepared almost to the letter as Queen Victoria's kitchen contemporaries did them. Her own chef Francatelli scamps on the sauce but elaborates with pardonable smugness his method for the whole entrée, and his rival Soyer of the Reform Club makes up for it by giving a recipe for the sauce alone that would stun modern gourmets.

Herewith I present them both, *chefs d'oeuvres* of two dashing culinary kings, flashing-eyed, soft-lipped prancing fellows if the engravings printed at their own expense in their two cookbooks are even half true.

Soyer's Sauce à la Financière

Put a wineglassful of sherry into a stewpan with a piece of glaze the size of a walnut, and a bay-leaf, place it upon the fire, and when it boils add a quart of demi-glace; let it boil ten minutes, keeping it stirred; then add twelve fresh blanched mushrooms, twelve prepared cock's-combs, a throat sweetbread cut in thin slices, two French preserved truffles also in slices, and twelve small veal forcemeat quenelles; boil altogether ten minutes, skim it well, thin it with a little consommé if desired, but it must be rather thick, and seasoned very palatably.

This is of course from *The Gastronomic Regenerator*, which the famous Reform Club's even more famous chef dedicated to the Duke of Cambridge in 1847. It can be assumed at our safe distance that the Queen's cook needed no lessons from the Club's, but even so Francatelli's sauce recipe is less interesting. His detailed method, though, for preparing the quail with and for the sauce is a fine prose poem to the God of Gastronomical Surfeit, and I give it here for modern pondering.

Francatelli's Quails à la Financière

Remove the bones entirely from eight fat quails, reserve the livers, and add to them half a pound of fat livers of fowl, with which prepare some force-meat, and stuff the quails with part of this; they must then be trussed in the usual manner, and placed in a stewpan with layers of fat bacon under them, a garnished faggot of parsley in the centre, and covered with layers of fat bacon; moisten with some wine mirepoix, *and braize them gently for about three-quarters of an hour. Prepare a rich Financière sauce, which must be finished with some of the liquor in which the quails have been braized. When about to send to table, warm the quails, drain and dish them up, garnish the centre with the Financière, pour some of the sauce around the entrée, and serve.*

This recipe is rather reminiscent of Brillat-Savarin's method for pheasant à la Sainte Alliance, although less pure, gastronomically speaking. He would, I think, have shuddered at applying it in no matter how simplified a form to quails, of which he wrote, "A man betrays his ignorance every time he serves one cooked otherwise than roasted or *en papillote*, for its aroma is most fragile, and dissolves, evaporates, and vanishes whenever the little creature comes in contact with a liquid."

It has always astonished and horrified me that this pretty wild bird, which Brillat-Savarin called "the daintiest and most charming" of all of them, should be so thoroughly unpleasant to clean, once killed. Its innards, supposedly nourished on the tenderest of herbs and grains, send out a stench that is almost insupportable, and hunters dread the moment when they must cope with it, in order to savor somewhat later one of the finest tastes in all the world.

The best of these that I have ever eaten were in Juárez, Mexico, in two shoddy, delightful "clubs" where illegal game was cooked by Chinese chefs, the quails grilled quickly over desert-bush coals, split open flat, and brought sizzling and charred to the table, innocent of grease or seasoning, and served with a dollop of strangely agreeable cactus-apple conserve. They were superb, thus unhampered.

A recipe I would follow if I could is the classical one for Quails in Ashes, *Cailles sous la Cendre*, a true hunters' rule, whose prime requisite is a fine log fire!

Each clean, emptied bird is wrapped in thickly buttered grape leaves and good bacon. (This is supposedly late summer, when the grain-fattened birds have fled before the guns to the high fertile meadows, just before the vineyards begin to turn gold.) Then they are enclosed in sturdy, buttered "parchment" paper, put in the hot ashes, and left there for a half hour or a little more, with fresher hotter cinders raked over them from time to time. When ready to be served, the paper is cut off, and the inward-reaching layers of bacon, grape leaf, and tender quail send out such a vapor, I know, as would rouse Lazarus.

H *is for*
Happy

. . . and for what kind of dinner is most often just that evanescent, unpredictable, and purely heaven-sent thing.

In general, I think, human beings are happiest at table when they are very young, very much in love, or very lone. It is rare to be happy in a group: a man can be merry, gay, keenly excited, but not happy in the sense of being free—free from life's cluttering and clutching.

When I was a child my Aunt Gwen (who was not an aunt at all but a large-boned and enormous-hearted woman who, thank God, lived next door to us) used to walk my little sister Anne and me up into the hills at sundown. She insisted on pockets. We had to have at least two apiece when we were with her. In one of them, on these twilight promenades, would be some cookies. In the other, oh, deep sensuous delight! would be a fried egg sandwich![1]

Nobody but Aunt Gwen ever made fried egg sandwiches for us. Grandmother was carefully protected from the fact that we had ever even heard of them, and as for Mother, preoccupied with a second set of children, she shuddered at the thought of such greasebound proteins with a thoroughness which should have made us chary but instead succeeded only in satisfying our human need for secrets.

The three of us, Aunt Gwen weighing a good four times what Anne and I did put together, would sneak out of the family ken whenever we could, into the blue-ing air, our pockets sagging and our spirits spiraling in a kind of intoxication of freedom, breathlessness, fatigue, and delicious anticipation. We would climb high above other mortals, onto a far rock or a fallen eucalyptus tree, and sit there, sometimes close as burrs and sometimes apart, singing straight through *Pinafore* and the Episcopal Hymn Book (Aunt Gwen was British and everything from contralto to basso profundo in the Whittier church choir), and biting voluptuously into our tough, soggy, indigestible and luscious suppers. We flourished on them, both physically and in our tenacious spirits.

Lone meals, which can be happy too, are perhaps the hardest to put on paper, with a drop of cyanide on their noses and a pin through their guts. They are the fleetingest of the gastronomical butterflies. I have known some. We all have. They are compounded in almost equal parts of peace, nostalgia, and good digestion, with sometimes an amenable touch of alcohol thrown in.

As for dining-in-love, I think of a lunch at the Lafayette in New York, in the front café with the glass pushed back and the May air flowing almost visibly over the marble tabletops, and a waiter named Pons, and a bottle of Louis Martini's Folle Blanche and moules more-or-less marinières but delicious, and then a walk in new black-heeled shoes with white stitching on them beside a man I had just met and a week later was to marry, in spite of my obdurate resolve never to marry again and my cynical recognition of his super-salesmanship. Anyone in the world could dream as well . . . being blessed . . .

Group happiness is another thing. Few of us can think with honesty of a time when we were indeed happy at table with more than our own selves or one other. And if we succeed in it, our thinking is dictated no matter how mysteriously by the wind, the wine, and the wish of that particular moment.

Now, for no reason that I consciously know of, I remember a lunch at the Casino at Berne, in Switzerland. I was with my father and mother, my husband, and a friend deep in his own murky moods but still attainable socially. We had driven there from Vevey, and we sat in the glass-enclosed bourgeois sparkle of the main dining room with a fine combination of tired bones and bottoms, thirst, hunger, and the effect of altitude.

I do not recall that we drank anything stronger than sherry before lunch, but we may have; my father, a forthright man who had edited a paper in the hard-liquor days when his Midwest village had fifteen saloons and three churches or thereabouts, may have downed a drink or two of Scotch, or the Bernese play on words, *ein Gift*, aptly called "poison" and made of half sweet vermouth and half any alcohol from vodka to gin.

Then, and this is the part I best remember, we had carafes of a rosé wine that was believed to be at its peak, its consummateness, in Berne, and indeed in that very room. Zizerser it was called. It came in the open café pitchers with the Federal mark at the top, naming the liquid content. It was a gay, frivolous color. It was poured into fine glasses (they were one of the many good things about that casino) from a height of two feet or so, and miracle! it foamed! It bubbled! It was full of a magic gas, that wine, which melted out of it with every inch of altitude it lost, so that when I took down a case of it and proudly poured it lakeside, in Vevey, it was merely a pink pretty drink, flat as flat. In Berne it was champagne. We drank deep.

So did our driver, François, and later when a frenzied-looking mountaineer waved back our car, we drove on with nonchalance along a cliff road above fabulous gorges, singing "Covered all over with Sweet Violets" and "Dir Heimat" (ensemble) and "Rover Was Blind but Brave" (my mother), until finally a rock about half as big as our enormous old Daimler sailed lazily down in front of us and settled a few feet from the engine.

We stopped in time.

Another mountaineer, with tiny stars of gold in his ear lobes to make him hear better, dropped into sight from the pine forest. Go back, go back, he cried. We are blasting a new road. You might have been killed. All right, all right, we said.

He lingered, under the obvious spell of our happiness. We talked. My father introduced my mother as the sweetest singer in Onawaiowa, which once she was. My husband breathed deeply, as if in sleep. My friend looked out over the plumy tree-tops and sighed for a lost love. François blinked in a surfeit of content. We all sat about, on felled branches and running boards, and drank some superlative cognac from an unlabeled bottle which my father had bought secretly from a Vevey wine merchant and brought along for just this important moment.

A couple more boulders drifted down and settled, dustily and noisily but without active danger, within a few feet of us.

The mountaineer sang three or four songs of his canton. Then, because of the Zizerser and mostly and mainly because we were for that one moment in all time a group of truly happy people, we began to yodel. My father, as a small-town editor, had the edge on us: he had practiced for years at the more unbridled of the local service-club luncheons and banquets. My mother found herself shooting off only too easily into *Aïda* and the more probable sections of *Parsifal*. My husband and even my friend hummed and buzzed, and I too buzzed and hummed. And François? He really yodeled, right along with the man from the mountains.

It was a fine thing. Whatever we had eaten at lunch, trout I think, went properly with the Zizerser, and we were full and we were happy, beyond the wine and the brandy, beyond the immediate danger of blasted boulders and cascading slides, beyond any feeling of foolishness. If we had lunched on milk and pap, that noontime in the Casino, we still would have felt the outer-world bliss that was ours, winy and full, on the Oberland mountainside that summer day.

It happened more than ten years ago, but if I should live a hundred and ten more I would still feel the freedom of it.

I

Aunt Gwen's Fried Egg Sandwiches

INGREDIENTS *(Physical)*

½ to 1 cup drippings   12 slices bread
6 fresh eggs   waxed paper

The drippings are very English, the kind poured off an unidentified succession of beef, mutton, and bacon pans, melted gradually into one dark puddle of thick unappetizing grease, which immediately upon being dabbed into a thick hot iron skillet sends out rendingly appetizing smells.

The eggs must be fresh, preferably brown ones, best of all freckled brown ones.

The bread must be good bread, no puffy, blanched, uniform blotters from a paper cocoon.

The waxed paper must be of honest quality, since at the corners where it will leak a little some of it will stick to the sandwich and in a way merge with it and be eaten.

INGREDIENTS *(Spiritual)*

These have been amply indicated in the text, and their prime requisite—Aunt Gwen herself would be the first to cry no to any further exposition of them. Suffice it that they were equal parts of hunger and happiness.

METHOD

Heat the drippings in a wide flat-bottomed skillet until they spit and smoke. Break in the eggs, which will immediately bubble around the edges, making them crisp and indigestible, and break their yolks with a fork and swirl them around, so that they are scattered fairly evenly through the whites. This will cook very quickly, and the eggs should be tough as leather.

Either push them to one side of the pan or remove them, and fry bread in the drippings for each sandwich, two slices to an egg. It too will send off a blue smoke. Fry it on one side only, so that when the sandwiches are slapped together their insides will turn soggy at once. Add to this sogginess by pressing them firmly together. Wrap them well in the waxed paper, where they will steam comfortably.

These sandwiches, if properly made and wrapped, are guaranteed, if properly carried in sweater or pinafore pockets, to make large oily stains around them.

Seasoning depends on the state of the drippings. As I remember Aunt Gwen's, they were such a "fruity" blend of last week's roast, last month's gammon, that salt and pepper would have been an insult to their fine flavor.

PRESCRIPTION

To be eaten on top of a hill at sunset, between trios of "A Wandering Minstrel I" and "Onward Christian Soldiers," preferably before adolescence and its priggish queasiness set in.

I *is for*
Innocence

. . . and its strangely rewarding chaos, gastronomically.

There is a great difference in my mind between innocence in this gourmand interpretation, and ignorance. The one presupposes the other, and yet a truly innocent cook or host is never guilty of the great sin of pretension, while many an ignorant one errs hideously in this direction.

Almost any man who is potentially capable of thus cheating his guests is also incapable of telling the truth to himself and will sneak a quick look into a primer of wine names, for instance, and then pretend that he knew all along to serve red wine with red meat or some such truism. His lie will betray his basic insecurity.

An innocent, on the other hand, will not bother to pretend any knowledge at all. He will, with a child's bland happiness, do the most God-awful things with his meals, and manage by some alchemy of warmth and understanding to make any honest gourmet pleased and easy at his table.

The best example of this that I can think of happened to me a few months ago.

I know a large, greedy, and basically unthinking man who spent all the middle years of his life working hard in a small town and eating in waffle shops and now and then gorging himself at friends' houses on Christmas Day. Quite late he married a large, greedy, and unthinking woman who introduced him to the dubious joys of whatever she heard about on the radio: Miracle Sponge Delight, Aunt Martha's Whipped Cheese Surprise, and all the homogenized, pasteurized, vitalized, dehydratized products intrinsic to the preparation of the Delights and the Surprises. My friend was happy.

He worked hard in the shop and his wife worked hard at the stove, her sinkside portable going full blast in order not to miss a single culinary hint. Each night they wedged themselves into their breakfast-bar-dinette and ate and ate and ate. They always meant to take up Canfield, but somehow they felt too sleepy. About a year ago he brought home a little set of dominoes, thinking it would be fun to shove the pieces around in a couple of games of Fives before she cleared the table. But she looked hard at him, gave a great belch, and died.

He was desperately lonely. We all thought he would go back to living in the rooming-house near the shop, or take up straight rye whisky, or at least start raising tropical fish.

Instead he stayed home more and more, sitting across from the inadequate little chromiumed chair his wife had died in, eating an almost ceaseless meal. He cooked it himself, very carefully. He listened without pause to her radio, which had literally not been turned off since her death. He wrote down every cooking tip he heard, and "enclosed twenty-five cents in stamps" for countless packages of Whipperoo, Jellerino, and Vita-glugg. He wore her tentlike aprons as he bent over the stove and the sink and the solitary table, and friends told me never, never, *never* to let him invite me to a meal.

But I liked him. And one day when I met him in the Pep

Brothers' Shopping Basket—occasionally I fought back my claustrophobia-among-the-cans long enough to go there for the best frozen fruit in town—he asked me so nicely and straightforwardly to come to supper with him that I said I'd love to. He lumbered off, a look of happy purpose wiping the misery from his big face; it was like sunlight breaking through smog. I felt a shudder of self-protective worry, which shamed me.

The night came, and I did something I very seldom do when I am to be a guest: I drank a sturdy shot of dry vermouth and gin, which I figured from long experience would give me an appetite immune to almost any gastronomical shocks. I was agreeably mellow and uncaring by the time I sat down in the chair across from my great, wallowing, bewildered friend and heard him subside with a fat man's alarming *puff!* into his own seat.

I noticed that he was larger than ever. You like your own cooking, I teased. He said gravely to me that gastronomy had saved his life and reason, and before I could recover from the shock of such fancy words on his strictly one-to-two syllable tongue, he had jumped up lightly, as only a fat man can, and started opening oven doors.

We had a tinned "fruit cup,"[1] predominantly gooseberries and obviously a sop to current health hints on station JWRB. Once having disposed of this bit of medical hugger-muggery, we surged on happily through one of the ghastliest meals I ever ate in my life. On second thought I can safely say, *the* ghastliest. There is no point in describing it, and to tell the truth a merciful mist has blurred its high points. There was too much spice where there should be none; there was sogginess where crispness was all-important; there was an artificially whipped and heavily sweetened canned-milk dessert where nothing at all was wanted.

And all through the dinner, in the small, hot, crowded room, we drank lukewarm Muscatel, a fortified dessert wine sold locally in gallon jugs, mixed in cheese-spread glasses with equal parts of a popular bottled lemon soda. It is incredible, but it happened.

I am glad it did. I know now what I may only have surmised theoretically before: there is indeed a gastronomic innocence, more admirable and more enviable than any cunning cognizance of menus and vintages and kitchen subtleties. My gross friend, untroubled by affectations of knowledge, served forth to me a meal that I was proud to partake of. If I felt myself at times a kind of sacrificial lamb, stretched on the altar of devotion, I was glad to be that lamb, for never was nectar poured for any goddess with more innocent and trusting enjoyment than was my hideous glass filled with a mixture of citric acid, carbon dioxide, and pure vinous hell for me. I looked into the little gray eyes of my friend and drank deep and felt the better for it.

He had not pretended with me nor tried to impress me. He knew I liked to eat, so he had cooked for me what he himself enjoyed the most. He remembered hearing somewhere that I liked wine with my meals, so he had bought "the mixings," as he knew them, because he wanted me to feel gay and relaxed and well thought of, there in his dear woman's chair, with her radio still blasting and her stove still hot. I felt truly grateful, and I too felt innocent.

I

My father, who was born within shouting distance of the back room of his parents' small-town newspaper office, and was making up forms on a tombstone when he was nine, and has been a small-town newspaperman for a good sixty years since, claims to have been served more fruit cup than any man alive.

He may well be right: he has gone to an unaccountable number of Chamber of Commerce Semi-Annual Luncheons, Get-Together Suppers, and service-club Annual Banquets, not to mention Father-Daughter Feeds, and gastronomical assemblies to Let-Us-Caponize-Our-Pullets Week, Be-Kind-to-the-Walnut-Pickers Month, and Better-Butter Year. And at a probable nine out of every ten of these feasts he has sat down, cold (unless previously warmed by a discreet stirrup cup *chez lui*), to a short-stemmed glass filled with a seemingly patented and changeless mixture of overcooked tinned fruits, always with a cherry lurking somewhere between its recommended place on top and the watery bottom.

Father mentions this dubious honor, world's champion of fruit-cup contemplaters, with a quiet, fatalistic pride. He says, when pressed, that he feels none the worse for the long siege, and that he infinitely prefers this gastronomical test to any other he can think of in the lexicon of small-town feastings.

Soups are impossible. The Ladies' Guilds and suchlike, which most often agree to serve the local merchants for a set weekly fee, are incapable, either in equipment or skill, of presenting a hot palatable broth to their contracted numbers, which may range from twenty to five hundred, always with a proportionate ten percent of unexpected delegations from neighboring towns.

Salads are universally shunned: the Ladies dislike them because they wilt and don't look pretty, and diners dislike them because the Ladies don't seem to know how to make them fit to swallow.

Any such outlandish and foreign appetizer as an inexpensive and stimulating canapé of something is rife with political, religious, and cultural suspicion, and therefore best left unconsidered.

There remains the fruit cup. It can be put on the tables anywhere from half an hour to half a day before the feast, depending on the weather. It looks, the Ladies say, "nice," no matter how long it has stood, and the best local cooks know to a fine drop how much of the canned liquid to allow to each cup so that it will stay moist but not too soupy. It comes in gallon tins, much cheaper and more generally successful than any fussy mixture of fresh local fruits. What is more, housewives who want to please husbands who have grown used to it in their business lives can make it just as well at home, from a can marked with some faintly varying version of the following: "diced Bartlett pears, diced yellow peaches, pineapple tidbits, best gooseberries, artificially colored, artificially flavored modified cherries in heavy syrup."

Almost any of these mentioned edibles (if indeed considered edible—there is some question about gooseberries) is worth a passing query, but I think the modified cherries have the finest ring of fantasy to them. What has modified them? And how?

To be truthful, I have no great enthusiasm for fruits as an appetizer, as a prelude to higher flavor (unless tomatoes be considered a fruit, which technically they are). I have eaten chilled slender slices of melon in the summertime, in Europe and in California, that were delicious, but no temptation to continue to anything else, which they were meant to be. Rather, I would have stopped with them, and sipped cold wine an hour longer with none but their own delicate flavor upon my tongue. In Italy I have eaten figs, as well as melons, served with prosciutto, ripe, seedy, overpowering figs warring with the salt challenge of the ham, and I have liked them very much. And Escoffier gives as an appetizer a recipe for chilled figs served peeled on a bed of green leaves and ice.

I still rebel.

Perhaps it is a latent hereditary revolt, handed on to me by my well-mannered, incredibly tolerant father. Perhaps if he were laid out on a psychoanalyst's couch, he would babble of fruit cups, gooseberries as green as the mayor, pineapple sharp as the advertiser who cut off his account last week after Father printed the story of his son's drunken-driving fine, peaches and pears and syrup as bland as the small-town diplomacy my sire has practiced for so long—and all of it served, and then eaten, with a common compassion, the good women in the kitchen, the good men bending over the banquet trestles, considering flood control, and rent control, and pest control—and fruit cup.

J is for
Juvenile dining

. . . and the mistakenness of adults who think that the pappy pabulum stuffed down their children's gullets is swallowed, when and if it is swallowed, with anything more than weak helplessness and a bitter if still subconscious acceptance of the hard fact that they must eat to survive.

I myself was fascinated witness to the first bite of so-called "solid food" my elder daughter took.

Quite aside from my innate conviction that she is unusually subtle and sensitive, I considered her at that moment undeniably *normal*, and felt that I was watching a kind of cosmic initiation to what, if I had anything to say about it, would be a lifetime of enjoyment of the pleasures of the table. I was depressed, then, to see such a thorough, bone-shaking, flesh-creeping shudder flash through her wee frame when the spoonful of puréed green beans touched her tongue, as I had known before only in the tragicomic picture of a hungover bindlestiff downing his morning shot of red-eye. She shook from top to toe in a real throe of revulsion. Then she looked at me, and speculation grew in her wide gaze.

I wondered in a kind of panic if perhaps true papillary bliss lay in a lifetime of bottle-feeding. While the child stared at me I ate a spoonful of her stuff, not to goad her into taking more of it but to see if I too would shudder. I did: it had a foully metallic taste, even to me whose tongue was perforce much duller than her innocent uncalloused one.

But she must eat puréed green beans, I thought, if I want her to flourish and go on to better things. So I took what was left in her silver porringer and put it in a porcelain bowl, feeling somewhat helplessly that thus I might curb the nasty taste of metal.

Perhaps I did; I'm not sure. I know that when I brought the dish back to my babe she opened her mouth, poker-faced, and ate everything with only a faint sigh to show her helplessness.

Since then, over some five years, she has progressed with a mixture of common sense and emotion through several stages of appreciation. She likes things with salt on them, feeling instinctively the stimulus of that abused flavoring (which I seldom allow her), and this morning when I asked her with clinical interest what she most loved to eat she told me without hesitation that it was potato chips. As far as I know she has never eaten one in her life. But she has heard me say how salty they are, and that, combined with the fact that she has also heard me say that I adore them (but don't eat them because they are hellishly fattening), made her answer like a flash that she adored them too.

She does not want *fat* things, too much sweet butter on her bread and such. She hates, with a real intensity, pepper; and I suppose she would react in the same clear-cut way to other hot seasonings, curry, for instance.

She does not like whisky or brandy for the same instinctively protective reasons, but she enjoys an occasional apéritif of Dubonnet or white wine with soda water (proportions about one to fifty, I would say), which she clicks against my glass with the proper *Salud* or *Santé* or *Na Zdarovia*.

She has the waistline of an especially slim bee and eats about six minuscule meals a day, for lack of space I suppose, and almost every day I give her one taste of something from the grown-up board, to prepare her, toughen her, indoctrinate her.

One time it is a nibble of Wisconsin Cheddar as big as a pin-head. She likes it. Another time it is a microscopic smear of Camembert or Liederkranz. She pulls away, shocked by its fine odor of putrescence, too decadent for her simplicity. I let her taste a Coke, knowing fatalistically that she must inevitably absorb them for social reasons. And it is the same with candy bars and grocery-store cakes and all that: I feel that I must harden her to their packaged onslaught rather than shield her from it, since she is to be a good, well-balanced American citizen.

So far the only thing in this category of preventive nutrition that she yearns for is a Popsicle, which she was once given by a well-meaning ranch hand and which in retrospect has acquired all the nostalgic beauty that I myself attribute to a truffled pâté I ate too many years ago during the Foire Gastronomique in Dijon.

As for the Cokes and cookies I use experimentally on her to accustom her to them, she is polite but largely uninterested; she will eat them, but ho-hum is the word. It is a different thing with "bought" bread. Most of the stuff that comes already sliced and in waxed paper she picks up, occasionally smells, and then puts quietly down again, no matter what strength of hunger gnaws at her.

Fortunately I can buy, more often than not, a brand of bread that is not only edible but good. It is brown as the ripe earth, nutty, moist, and inescapably honest. My daughter feels this honesty the way she would feel terror at a madman's leer, with an intuitive knowledge. When she has not known I was watching, I have seen her sniff a crust of this good stuff and smile, unthinking as a puppy but absolutely right.

And I have thought sadly how far we have come from our forefathers in Latvia or Sicily or Cornwall who once so honored bread that if they dropped a piece of it on the floor they begged its pardon. In our country today it is in a sorry waxbound servitude, so weak that it must be reinforced with chemicals, so tricked-out that a hungry dog or cat will not eat the puffy stuff unless it is actually starving.

My child likes a kind of pattern to her meals: I put raisins in rows, instead of willy-nilly, on a slice of buttered toast, or rounds of banana in an X or an A over the top of her applesauce[1]—A is for Anne, and X is, but naturally, for X-citing! Now and then, pure gastronomical fillip, there is a faint dash of cinnamon, a touch of nutmeg.

In five years she has been sick only once, in the good old English sense of the word, and that was psychosomatic rather than digestive, when a brush fire threatened us.

She seems to have a constant and lively speculation about taste and a truly "curious nose," which reassures me when I remember her first instinctive shudder, and which keeps me watching, trying, testing, and always using my wits to avoid havoc. I want her to have a keen palate, inquisitive but never tyrannical. I want her to be able to eat at least one taste of anything in the world, from Beluga caviar to porcupine grilled with locusts, with social impunity and a modicum of inquisitive gusto.

I want her to shun such gluttonous excesses as those of two small boys we know who, like half-starved beasts, wait with an unhealthy intensity for the aftermath of their parents' cocktail parties and then drain every glass and strip the messed hors d'oeuvres trays of every crumb of shriveled anchovy and withered olive.

I want her, on the other hand, to avoid such back-to-the-earth gourmandism as is betrayed by the earnest addicts of stone-ground, hand-trampled, nature-cured (and inevitably mildewed and weevilly) buckwheat groats and such, who, I find, are pretty dull once they have been fed—and/or eaten.

I am doing all I can to turn Anne into a sentient, intelligent, voluptuously restrained gastronomer, with a clear recognition of the odds of modern "improvements": pasteurization, dehydration, *et al.*; with firm resolves never to make her eat anything, from oatmeal gruel to escargots à la mode de Bourgogne,[2] and never to hurry her; and with a constant excitement and a growing conviction that I am giving her something much more precious than Great-Aunt Jennie's topaz parure.

I

My mother used to make the best applesauce I have ever eaten, and the only recipe I have found that uses her "trick" is in Marion Harland's *Common Sense in the Household: A Manual of Practical Housewifery*, which was published in 1871 and which by a completely unstrange coincidence belonged to my mother's mother.

My mother's trick, thus obviously passed on to her, is to stir in a plump lump of honest butter just as the mixture is to be removed from the stove. It is, to my knowledge, infallible—that is, if you like applesauce that is somewhat lumpy, never, never, *never* puréed, never, never, *never* flavored with vanilla or lemon-zest as if it were a sissified pudding; it is a lightly cooked mixture of pared apple quarters and brown sugar, doused, once in its bowl, with a bit of powdered cinnamon, no more.

But, ah, that rich Victorian touch of the butter pat! Ah, the good, almost grainy texture, and the forthright ugly color of it in a sauce dish, with milk alongside or a slab of hot gingery molasses cake! Ah, nothing but *applesauce*—even if Mrs. Harland did put her recipe among the Meat Garnishes and say, with her habitual firm authority, "It is the invariable accompaniment of roast pork—or fresh pork cooked in any way."

2

Many people eat snails, in every fashion from the most primitive one of burning the bushes upon which they feed and then

sucking them hot and roasted from the ashy shells, to the most
intricate, complete with specifically shaped brushes for scrub-
bing the involuted little houses and special forks for plucking
them, correctly starved, fed, starved, washed, cooked, sauced,
and finally broiled, from those same lovely shelters.

I cannot decide whether the idea of eating a snail is intuitively
repulsive: by the time I myself was confronted by a plate of
them, *chez* Crespin in Dijon, in about October of 1929, I had
been conditioned by enough other gastronomical tests to be
able to meet them with equanimity. I looked around the plain,
pleasant little room, and at the end of it crossed glances with a
visiting provincial, a woman about sixty with the full, coarse,
ribald, moody face of a real Burgundian, happy that night at
least. We looked at one another, and as we looked she slowly
picked up three or four shells from the sizzling plate in front of
her, tipped the hot garlicky juice from each one into her mouth,
and then swabbed at it with a morsel of her crusty bread. I felt
very young and glad for the lesson, and did likewise, with only
a faint and final nod to whatever nascent prohibitions against
the beasts themselves might have stayed with me.

Since then I have eaten snails prepared in perhaps five or six
other ways and have not really liked them; they are basically a
tough bite and need some such heady treatment as the one they
get in Burgundy to interest me. Oddly enough I cannot find a
recipe, à la bourguignonne, that sounds quite the way it should
to produce those tender-green shimmering things that used to
be piled in Dijon store windows in cool weather, prepared with
such skill and patience to sell for a penny or so apiece, and then
be taken home and heated on their special little dimpled platters
to please the Côte d'Or gourmandizers and gourmets.

The nearest I can come to it is in, of all things, a collection of
Bordeaux recipes! And it calls for minced mushrooms, which I
feel pretty sure the Dijon snails did not have, and "a pinch of
garlic" where they were dizzy with it.

But the slow, finicky preparation of the snails, the fasting, the washings, the boiling with a little sack of charcoal in the water—all that sounds correct; and then the final aromatic mixture of herbs and sweet butter, which is packed smoothly over the snail, by now returned to its clean shell—that too has the rightful ring.

I know, though, that my young daughters would not like it—yet. They must wait many more years. It took me twenty or so, California being so far removed from France, and they perforce cannot have the indoctrination that made my friends Doudouce and Plume such seasoned tasters at the ages of ten and twelve, when I helped them pluck the snails from twigs and suffered with them through the tedium of preparation, in Dijon so long ago. Plume is now buried, and Doudouce disappeared, but the aura of true gastronomy that surrounded them is still strong in my mind and heart. I hope that my own children will know a little of it.

K *is for*
Kosher

. . . and for a few reasons that the dietary laws laid down by Jehovah to Moses in 1490 B.C. have rightly been called "one of the best economic regimes ever made public," gastronomically as well as otherwise.

These interdictions, which except to the orthodox Jews have come to mean very little beyond borscht and blintzes in any restaurant which displays the Star of David, are puzzling mainly because so few people really know them (including a great many modern Jews, who are astonished to learn that they can read them easily in Leviticus, the Third Book of Moses in the Old Testament—and very good reading it is, for anyone with a gourmet's "curious nose").

The complex rituals for the butchering and inspection of meats by properly trained men need bother no one, since these are taken care of by experts before food is bought and prepared for the table; but the ancient, sensible, good rules for cookery, to be followed or at least pondered on, are best told as Moses told them to his people more than a thousand years before the greatest Jew frightened the Romans in Jerusalem and then, after the Passover feast, died, perhaps to save them.

Pragmatism, of course, often triumphs over religious principles, as when, in G. B. Stern's *The Matriarch*, Babette Rakonitz inadvertently discovered the excellence of ham and managed to enjoy it for many a long year by pretending not to know what she was eating. It is easy to reason as Babette did, when wealth and wanderings have turned people willy-nilly into tolerant cosmopolites like the Rakonitzes. And there are many Jews like them.

It is the poorer ones, the oppressed, who have held fiercely and loyally to the ceremonial laws bound round and round them, who centuries after their nation disappeared, to rise again, stand unshakable as a people of great religious faith. It is an astonishing and moving thing that after so many flights from terror, after so many vigils in strange lands, many Jews still feast and fast as Moses told them to.

It is exciting, gastronomically, to recognize the influence of their wanderings in their wealth of dishes: olives and oil from Spain and Portugal; German sweet-and-sour stews; cucumbers, herrings, butter cakes, and grain rolls called bolas from the hospitable Dutchmen; fishes stewed and stuffed, and fremal soup made with goose drippings, from Poland; from Russia and Rumania the blintzes, the buckwheat groats called kasha and puddings called Kugel, the sweet heaviness of fruit compotes and preserves, and borscht thin or thick, hot or cold, any time of the clock or calendar.[1]

But it is not the international flavor of the Jewish cuisine that makes it really exciting; rather, it is the fact that many dietary and ceremonial laws have of necessity evolved a peculiar art of substitution, disguise, and even trickery (a trickery which has nothing to do with dishonesty, as was the case in rich Babette's delicate gluttony, but which is one solely of flavorings and spicings).

Fish is a much used dish of the Jews because of the many prohibitions about preparing and eating meats. Highly seasoned salmon, for instance, is one of the main dishes for the Sabbath, when all cooking is forbidden, since it can be made the day before and served delectably in a hundred ways when it is cold. Fish is convenient too, because there is no prohibition against cooking a cold-blooded animal with cream or cheese or any other milk products.

Meat is usually served only once daily in Jewish households that can afford it at all, but even so, relatively few vegetables are eaten in most orthodox homes, since they cannot be prepared with butter or cream at any meal containing meat, and the cooks are therefore not educated to cope with them. They are eaten more by the poor people in soups than by the wealthier classes, although salads are more in favor than they were even a few years ago.

In a city like New York the number of children from strict Jewish families is enormous and the public-school teachers have to adjust many of their courses to that fact. In Domestic Science, for instance, where little girls are taught the rudiments of cooking, it can become a serious emotional problem if kosher rules are violated, even unwittingly. The same is true in school cafeterias, where children face alienation from their parents if they "forget" and eat both meat and ice cream at lunch.

Fortunately there are a great many feasts to be observed by good Jews, but there are also alarming numbers of strict fasts. A few of them, like the Fast of Esther which precedes the Feast of Purim, are observed now only by the very religious, but Yom Kippur, the Day of Atonement, will be a period of purification and reflection as long as the world rolls, wherever a Jew may find himself.

There are semi-fasts too, such as a nine-day period in the summer heat when no meat should be eaten: a simple, dietetically sound rule to protect any wandering or ill-housed people, whether in the desert of Arabia a thousand years ago or in a New York tenement next August!

The rules for keeping Passover properly are many, and to a Gentile are mysterious as well as very confusing. The most bothersome prescription is the one that no utensil which has touched even a crumb of leavened bread can be used for eight days. This means that separate sets of dishes are needed, and that all the table silver and cutlery must be sterilized.

·To "kasher" correctly (which means in Hebrew to make right or fit), red-hot stones are plunged into a kettle of boiling water and the various articles also immersed in it. They can be used when Passover has finished for that year, but must be kashered again before the next holiday. The special sets of table dishes are usually carefully wrapped and stored in a place where there is not even the faintest danger of their being polluted by the presence of leaven.

As a result of this and other kasher rules a strict orthodox family should have four complete sets of tableware: duplicate Passover sets, one for meat meals and one for dairy meals!

As for the house, it is scrubbed to the tiniest mousehole before Passover, to avoid such dangers as even a forgotten cake crumb might cause.

Passover dishes are probably the most interesting of any in the Jewish cuisine because of the lack of leaven and the resulting challenge to fine cooks. There are all kinds of torten and almond cakes and puddings, and an infinity of uses for mazzah or matzos: matzo klos, or dumplings, cakes and puddings of the matzo meal. Everything is doubly rich, as if to compensate for the lack of leaven, and clarified goose and chicken fat, and beef drippings carefully excluding suet, are used most artfully.

And it is thus that old Moses looked after his children, as well as in his bluntly realistic attempts to protect them from pollution and decay, dietetic as well as spiritual, in their wanderings through the hot, filthy countries of the ancient world: he made them see to it that the vessels for their feasting were sterile, freed from most of their omnipresent bacteria by the ceremony, at once mystical and practical, of kashering.

He forbade them to eat any kind of leaven, that fine proving ground for digestive bubbles.

He let them soothe their starved nerves and muscles at least once yearly with a wise unguent of fat, fat from the goose and even, most carefully, from the cow . . . and as any refugee from today's Europe knows, that is balm indeed, for hungering people who have had no fat at all for too long a time become moody, shiver easily, and grow sick.

Moses let his people lie back, now and then, upon whatever kind of couch they could find, and eat and eat. Even today, at Passover, they eat well if they eat at all, and woes are forgotten in the pleasures of the table, for if the Mosaic laws are rightly followed, no man need fear true poison in his belly, but only the results of his own gluttony.

I

The taste for borscht and the prejudices thereof can involve as many personal quirks as a recipe for hangovers. I have ceased to take them very seriously, for, after years of listening worshipfully to one famous comedian swear that he would eat borscht at only one restaurant in the whole world, where it was prepared magnificently and as it *should* be, I went to that restaurant, ordered that borscht, and found it a pale, watery, and indeed completely dishonest shadow of what I myself, unfamous uncomedian, think good borscht should be.

I believe that it is one of the best soups in the world. It can be hot, cold, thick, thin, rich, meager—and still be good. It can be easy or intricate to make.

Some people like it hot, with boiled beef in it, or quarters of cabbage (the variations on cabbage alone are almost infinite: chopped, minced, quartered, whole, on and on).

Some people like it cold, with chilled sour cream, poured over a steaming hot boiled potato in the middle of the plate.

Some people like grated fresh beets in it, and some like nothing at all, just the clear red consommé, and of course the cream.

Some people like little poached forcemeat balls in it.

Some people, apparently, like my comedian-friend, like it bad.

And then again there is the aspect of its sourness. Should it be fermented beets that give it its own peculiar sharpness, or fresh sliced beets in honest vinegar? Is it a heinous gastronomical sin to use the handier fresh lemon juice or vinegar instead of citric acid crystals from the corner drugstore? Should you spit it out and stalk from the table if it contains no sour taste at all, but rather the bland smoothness of a Little Borscht that can only be Polish if you are Russian, Russian if you are Finnish, and so on?

Well, I like it two ways the best, and these are they, one cold and easy to make, the other hot and comparatively complicated:

Cold Summer Borscht

1 *quart vegetable juice*	½ *to ¾ cup good vinegar*
1 *pint strong stock (canned*	1 *thinly sliced onion*
consommé is all right)	*salt, pepper, and so on*
1 *can sliced beets with juice*	

I say "and so on" because some people like a touch of clove or kümmel. The vegetable juice can be tinned or what is saved from pressure-cooking.

Pour the liquids into a casserole containing the canned sliced beets, their juice, the sliced onion, and the seasoning. Chill for 12 hours or more. Strain off the liquids and serve very cold with sour cream—and hot potatoes if desired.

Hot Winter Borscht

16 young beets	handful of parsley sprigs
2½ cups good vinegar	2 bay leaves
3 tablespoons butter or chicken fat	salt, pepper
2 sweet onions	3 tablespoons flour
4 young carrots	3 quarts rich beef stock

Scrape and wash the beets and put 12 of them through the coarse meat grinder. Cover with the vinegar for several hours. Melt the fat, add the onions and carrots which have been coarsely ground, the chopped parsley, the bay leaves, and seasoning. Stir until golden, add half the flour, brown all well, then stir in the rest of the flour. Drain the ground beets thoroughly, saving ½ to 1 cup of the vinegar, and add them to the braised vegetables. Add the stock. Let simmer a half hour or until the vegetables are tender. Grate on a cheese grater the four remaining beets, mix them with the vinegar, and add to the soup five minutes before serving. Little sausage balls poached in boiling water can be added, and of course an accompanying bowl of sour cream is necessary.

L is for
Literature

. . . and the banquets it can serve forth, from the gorgeously photographed Spamola sur Bun à la mode de Fourth-of-July of a present-day advertisement to the phosphorescent elegance of a courtesan's memoirs, in which every dish at her table possesses, at least in legend, a special phallic importance.

There is no question that secondhand feasting can bring its own nourishment, satisfaction, and final surfeit. More than one escaped war prisoner has told me of the strange peacefulness that will come over a group of near-famished men in their almost endless talk of good food they remember and wish to eat again. They murmur on and on, in the cells or the walled yards, of pies their sisters used to make for them, and of the way Domenico in Tijuana grilled bootleg quail, and of the pasta at Boeucc' in prewar Milan. They swallow without active pain the prison's maggotty bread and watery soup, their spiritual palates drowned in a flood of recalled flavor and warmth and richness.

If they had books, they would be reading their banquet. For want of them they talk it, voluptuously repetitious, unconsciously fighting against the death of their five senses, without which they would indeed be death-condemned.

The men outside the walls are not so immediately menaced, but there are many of us who have found something of the same sensuous relief from our invisible and private prisons in gastronomical literature.

Given the fact that almost every gastronomer has some kind of literary predilection, it is amusing and interesting to speculate on the whys and whens of such a love. I know one man, for instance, who for fairly obvious reasons collects only political menus, from Julius Caesar's to Harry Truman's; and another who for equally obvious reasons has little curiosity about any meal that has been served outside a brothel, to anyone but a whore or a whorer.

As for me, I sometimes think wistfully that it would be pleasant to be able so completely to limit myself! I have too much to read.

I have a fat pile of menus, actual ones dating from 1929 and book ones for the past five thousand years. Among them are the last dinner served *chez* Foyot, the ink already very faded, and an illuminated parchment limned by George Holl in San Francisco, the gold still bright although the round, witty gourmet is now gone, and a smudged paper from a Nazi *Bierstube* in Mexico, and another from a Loyalist café in Zurich where we drank out of bottles like udders, in squirts from the little glass dugs, as in a Hemingway story.

And there are so many books!

Why can I not limit myself to gastronomical novels, to *Hotel Imperial* by Arnold Bennett and *Work of Art* by Sinclair Lewis and all the stuff about hotels by Ludwig Bemelmans; or Huysmans and Saltus and Petronius and all those boys, new and old, who wrote of the excesses; or . . . or . . . or Virginia Woolf who wrote perhaps better than anyone in the Western world about the feeling of being a little drunk, or of being a hostess, in books like *The Waves* and *To the Lighthouse*? Why not make it that simple?

Or why not just cookery books? Why do I not just have what I think are the best work manuals and read them carefully when I need them (which I do constantly)? But no: I have everything from Mrs. Simon Kander's *Settlement Cook Book*, through all of Sheila Hibben, to the latest throwaways from baking powder and refrigerator companies, with their flossy culinary triumphs in full Kodachrome. I have them in rows and piles. Fortunately I also have the common sense to limit my working manuals to a maximum of twelve inches of shelf space. But the rest!'—they go on for countless feet, through European titles and Hawaiian and regional, through Suzanne Roukhomovsky and Trader Vic and André Simon, some of them good and a lot of them absolutely phony except for perhaps one invaluable recipe or hint.

And then the other books, the ones I have kept because they are bound in shagreen or mottled with age or smudged with the adolescent gorgings of boarding school! All have a gastronomical significance, some of them to no other human being but myself. They mean exoticism, or respect, or gluttony. Perhaps they should be shed at regular intervals, like a skin. But they sit safely on my shelves, a strange company bolstered by nostalgia, curious indeed, and a dead giveaway to anyone equally curious to know their owner.

I do believe sincerely that a gastronomical library, if it is sternly limited, is more significant than mine could ever be. That is, I think a collection of menus from the Regency to the First Republic or vice versa, as served in one town or one district, say Dijon or Seine-et-Oise, might prove to be intensely interesting to gourmets of the whole world. It might even have a fine building erected around it, and provide bookwormish nourishment for a score of dyspeptic curators. As for my own magpie collection, it can do little but bewilder.

Few but I can ever know, or care, why this particular frayed paper-bound edition of Paul Reboux's *Plats du Jour* means high zest and adventure in Burgundy in 1930. Perhaps no man in the world speaks truthfully who says he knows where my one-shilling copy of *Farmhouse Fare* came from, and why its recipe for Butter Brine brings me close to weeping. And how about *Notes on a Cellar Book* and why I keep this new shiny vulgar edition rather than the "first" I gave away? George Saintsbury would know. I know. But it does not matter in the least that no one else does, not at least to me.

I look at my crammed shelves and feast with artful reflection, for no meal is good that cannot be reflected upon with pleasure. It comforts me to know, in this distracted world, that thanks to my motley library I could be well fed in the worst of this world's distracted prisons.

I

There is no better antidote for me, when I have perforce read too many modern recipes, quasi- (or should I say queasy?) practical or purely fluffy, than a quiet backward look.

The English and American receipts of a hundred years ago, in Mrs. Beeton or Marion Harland, are hardly less removed from today's standards of goodness than Elizabethan formulas, and even the proper order of service at mealtime sounds strange, and proportionately refreshing and stimulating, in the middle-class cookery books I have mentioned, and in the higher flying lexicons like Soyer's *The Gastronomic Regenerator* and Simpson's *System of Cookery*, destined for aristocratic kitchens but most certainly peeked at by many a modest housewife of the early nineteenth century.

The jump back from Victoria to James the First is easy

enough, once having taken the greater one between today's manuals and Marion Harland's and Soyer's and suchlike. There, fortunate accident, opens *The Closet of Sir Kenelm Digby, Knight*, one of the most tantalizing and robust and in a way mysterious cookbooks ever written, except, perhaps, *The Deipnosophists* of Athenaeus.

Digby was an arch-romanticist, the "special friend of queens," an experimenter from his youngest days in the connection between what people eat and what they die of, from plague to poison. And the recipes, starting with "Take one Measure of Honey" for his Metheglin and ending ". . . it is a beautiful and pleasant Liquor" for his Conserve of Roses, are full of weird delight. The one quickest to hand, of countless such, is called

A Herring-Pye

Put great store of sliced onions, with Currants and Raisins of the Sun both above and under the Herrings, and store of Butter, and so bake them.

I read this cookery rule and then sit back, trying to taste with my mind's tongue the fantastic product of it (to me here and now, that is fantastic), a baked dish of onions, raisins, butter, and fish. I cannot. And then I go still further back, as far as the plumed decadence of Rome, remote from such Elizabethan vigor as Sir Kenelm Digby always showed, and yet blunt as his.

I read of sauces and bird-pyes, or of the intricacies of perfumed roasted fig-pecker breasts, or of pâté made from almond-stuffed white geese, or of

Garum (400 B.C.)

Place in a vessel all the insides of fish, both large fish and small. Salt them well. Expose them to the air until they are completely rotted. Drain off the liquid that comes from them, and it is the sauce garum.

This recipe, ugly and simple, is in its own way salutary against the onslaughts of marshmallow-vegetable-gelatin salads and such which smile at me in Kodachrome from current magazine advertisements. It can act, and indeed it does, as a kind of gastronomical purge, and I find myself turning much oftener than I need to, and perhaps with much more relief than I am justified in feeling, to the bygone receipts, the flummeries and syllabubs and pastes, of cooks now comfortably past hunger.

M *is for*
Monastic

. . . and for what happens when men become monks—at table, I hasten to add!

It seems to me that too much has been written about the dogged pleasures that can be savored by any knowing gourmet who sits down alone to his own idea of culinary excellence. Lucullus is called on far too often to bolster such solitary morale, and many a man who secretly yearns to join the nearest roistering group has smugly comforted himself by remembering how, one rare time when the great Roman general dined alone, he chided his chef for a slight feeling of hit-or-miss slapdashery in the menu. "But My Lord" (or Your Excellency or however anyone as rich as Lucullus was addressed some two thousand yers ago) "has no guests tonight," the poor dolt stammered, "and therefore . . ."

And then enough was said, for the fabulously skilled gastronomer shrugged coldly and remarked, "But tonight—tonight Lucullus dines with Lucullus!"

Yes, what comfort that cruel reproach has been to countless lonely but still normally hungry souls! They have sat back, in worldwide beaneries called everything from Le Roy Gourmet to Ye Kat's Meow, and hoped devoutly that they looked as blandly gourmandish as they wished they felt.

Some cities make this solitary public act much easier to accomplish than do others. It is apparently impossible for a man to dine alone with dignified enjoyment in Los Angeles, for example, except perhaps at a Thrift-i-Save drugstore counter, which automatically cancels out the dignity if not the enjoyment. I have yet to see any normal Southern California male go willingly by himself to an eating house and consume an intelligent meal easily and pleasurably.

On the other hand San Francisco has many restaurants where men seem to go not merely to staunch the wounds of their immediate appetite, but to sit alone and savor without chit-chat what has been set before them. There are places like Sam's and Jack's and Tadich's, often with mousy-looking curtained booths upstairs which in the main are *not* filled with the expected willing damsels and their sexually hungry escorts, but with calm-faced lawyers and bankers and vintners and sea captains, sitting miraculously by themselves, reading Elizabethan sermons and sonnets over the intricacies of a cracked crab's shell.

When I was last in Paris and London, they were like that, and will be again, I think.

But no matter how much help a place may give, men dining alone in public do not often find the ease and elegance they wish for. And as for their private gastronomical patterns, they are fantastic! For one famed celibate whose Filipino houseboy understands not only the intricacy of a soufflé au Grand Marnier but the precise and utterly precious moment at which to serve it, there are a hundred, a thousand, myriad men who are caught in the drab toils of modern moneys, and cannot afford such escapism.

They must live alone, for one reason or another. They learn countless ugly little tricks for such an existence, which add to the hateful pattern. They gradually forget Lucullus and lean on one good meal a week, with the rest filled in by snatched bottles of milk and grabbed drugstore ham-on-ryes. Now and then they let a girl grill them a steak in her kitchenette, which they would not let her pay for in a restaurant for obtusely virile reasons. But in general they prefer to survive in solitude.[1] Quite often they find themselves in a position similar to that of a friend of mine, who is aptly named Monk.

He was then about twenty-eight, which sounds young to some of us, but he was much older than most of the other students at the university where he was writing his doctor's thesis. He had very little money, and thanks to family troubles and an occasional irresistible urge for pretty girls, he found himself living on a food purse which had dwindled within a few months from seventy-five cents a day to about twelve. This happened to him in 1939, when it meant twice as much cash as ten years later, but even so he was hard put to it to sleep for the way his guts cried out and warbled to him in the night.

He was not alone in his hunger: there have been many such students who later grew fat as college presidents, and they tipped him off to such timeworn tricks as serving at fraternity banquets and eating the scraps. But Monk was finicky, and out of pure finickiness his belly protested at such untidy snatchings.

Then he made a deal with a hash house for one meal a day, everything he could eat, in return for washing plates. It was not right: the black greasiness underfoot wiped out any pleasure he may have found in the sparkling countertops of the little joint, and again he was racked with sickness.

It seemed to color not only his immediate eagerness for life but also his politics and even his lovemaking, and he realized that he must ignore the common ways of such poverty as his and devise his own plan. He was an intelligent man, although dulled and warped by hunger, and he deliberately lived another week on scraps in order to save a dollar or so to buy himself one pot, one plate, one spoon, and one fork. He did not need a knife, recognizing fatalistically that he would never cook anything that needed to be cut, anything like a steak . . . a chop. . . .

He arranged to use the back of his landlady's stove two or three times a week. She would have been more than glad to see him in her kitchen every day, but by now his monastic approach to life had spread from the table to the bed, and he withdrew with discreet relief from many such snagtoothed and fumy invitations.

He made himself a stew on Saturdays and Wednesdays. It had good things in it, which he bought just at closing time in the big public markets. It smelled good. It tasted good. He did not languish on it, he grew strong and sparkling.

The important part of the story is not that he continued to flourish, but that he stopped. One day he realized, alone in his odorous little back room with his empty plate before him, that he had at first, a few weeks earlier, eaten nicely from it with his fork. Then for a few weeks he had spooned up his food. And then one day he found himself very neatly, very thoroughly, licking the plate clean to save the bother of washing it three flights below!

He was flabbergasted. He sat back and thought about it. In some ways this licking was a logical act: no other soul but him would eat from the plate and therefore it was not contaminated by his doglike behavior. Also, it saved some of his jealously husbanded strength for his studies. Moreover, such secret washing protected him from the sly-eyed woman in the kitchen, which also kept some energy for other things. But he was horrified nevertheless.

Quietly he took the plate up and broke it over his knee. He

went down to the kitchen and gave the rest of his stew to a family of blue kittens which had lately emerged from the back alley.

Then he took three dollars and eleven cents, which he had counted on for the rest of the month, gastronomically, and he called his favorite girl, who was majoring in Dramatic Diction but enunciated his own language with great clarity on at least one important subject.

And the next morning he felt so much more energetic than he had for several months that he applied for, and immediately got, a fat job as a laboratory assistant. What happened to him later really should not happen to a rising physicist, but at least it had very little to do with monasticism, culinary or otherwise!

I

The things men come to eat when they are alone are, I suppose, not much stranger than the men themselves. I myself have concocted more than one weird dish when I felt I was unobserved and therefore inviolate.

A writer years ago told me of living for five months on hen mash. He said he felt fine at the end and was fatter in his purse than he could possibly have been otherwise, and that the only eggs he had laid were on magazine editors' desks. And if you study, instead of a cookbook, the requisite ingredients of any packaged food that is supposed to keep furred or feathered creatures in good shape, and even increase their usefulness, you will see the fantastic lengths to which cooks go, whether they be purveyors to hens and puppies or, at the other end of the gastronomical scale, royal chefs nourishing princes and prime ministers. Where one will specify three dozen ortolans, twelve large fresh truffles, and sauce Espagnole, the other will require calcium carbonate, bone meal, and fish liver oil in even fussier proportions.

I do not know what political reactions might ensue if a good honest dog biscuit were served, no matter how tricked out with this and that, at a state banquet, but from what little I have seen most animals would turn away from the overspiced mixtures put upon regal or diplomatic plates.

Myself, if I must choose, I would take the hen mash, the dog meal, for every day, with promise of a respite now and then, rather than daily ordeals of rich tricky nothingness. My palate might faint, but my bones would not, and, being alive, I must consider those bones and their uses, and the flesh thereon.

The phosphorescence that lurks upon the very breath of well-fed sophisticates, subtle mélange of béchamel, Seconal capsules, and bismuth, is not for me. I would, having measured my powers and my capacities, settle for many a monastic feeding of my physical cells, and then in the resultant glow of well-being sample a very occasional snail, truffle, pâté, pheasant Souvaroff, bombe Trocadéro, diplomate au kirsch. A time-to-time savoring of Lucullus's choicest fare, the kind he would serve in his Apollo room, has never harmed anyone who knew enough to sight his landmarks and recognize where he was. And on the other side of the medal, a "scouring of the maw" is something that Lucullus himself would recommend, a ritual not necessarily painful, which the most devout gourmets recognize as healthful.

Perhaps the best of such refreshers that I know, at least in its obvious results, is one described to me by a man who lives a life of innumerable Scotches at the Ritz, uncountable bisques and pâtés and tournedos, too many bottles of Château Lafitte (if that be possible), and all for reasons more professional than voluptuous. His antidote is good: once a month, or oftener if he can, he retires, in the full sense of the word, to his own privacy, in this case a two-room hotel apartment. He bathes slowly, cov-

ers himself softly, and lies back upon a couch, the inevitable
manuscripts at one side of him for possible scanning (but with
the telephone turned off), and at the other side a little table upon
which waits the following medicine, to be taken slowly:

Strengthening Prescription
for Monastic Supper

1 *small loaf crusty sourdough bread*	1 *stick sweet butter, a quarter pound or so*
1 *fresh but ripe piece of Gorgonzola or blue cheese*	1 *bottle Chianti or Tipo Red*

This menu presupposes a certain ease and dictates a definite
peacefulness. Better that than madness, digestive as well as social, and no more unattainable!

N *is for*
Nautical

. . . and inevitably for nostalgia, in my own alphabet. Dinners aboard ship have a special poignancy for me, partly because I have not sailed anywhere since I went with the *Normandie* on her last fateful crossing, but mostly because I have always been in love at sea, so that each bite I took was savored with an intensity peculiar to the moment. I think I am not alone in this particular juxtaposition of two words for *N*.

The first time I ever rode a ship it was deep down in the shuddering guts of it, so that dining room silver and china jangled tinnily on the calmest day—another coupling of two letters: *S* for Student Third rather than Steerage. It was smart to hop the Atlantic thus cheaply and uncomfortably in 1929, and a great many bored travelers who could afford A-deck accommodations titillated themselves by rubbing elbows with errant priests and broken-down fan dancers and even students in the renovated holds of a dozen enormous liners (mine was the *Berengaria*).

I myself was happily dazed with love, but I do remember one priest, one dancer, three medical students, and most of all one incongruously proper middle-class plump Englishwoman who had nothing to do with anyone at all and seemed nonexistent except three times a day in the dining room. Then it was that she became immortal, at least for me. With one blind regal stare she picked up the large menu, handed it to the apparently hypnotized waiter, who hovered over her and almost ignored the seven other passengers at our table, and said "Yes."

It seems to me, when I try to be reasonable about it, that she must surely have said, "Yes, pastries," or "Yes, soups." But all I can remember is "Yes." All I can remember is sitting for long periods watching her, when I should rightly have been playing shuffleboard or any other of the games connected with my first honeymoon, while she ate slowly, silently, right through the menu.

Surely it must have been all the soups one meal, and all the roasts another: no human being could eat every dish mentioned on a ship's carte du jour, not even in Student Third where kippered snacks and spiced onions took the place of First Class caviar and bouchées à la Pompadour. But as far as I can say, that woman did. What is more, the waiter seemed to enjoy it almost as much as she; he would hover breathlessly behind her with a dish of apple trifle and a plate of plum heavies while she chewed on through her chocolate sponge with one hand and cut at the crust of an apricot tart with the other.[1]

One day of comparative roughness, when the silver and china clashed noisily to the ocean's roll instead of jingling to the engine's shudderings, I sat almost alone in the room with this relentless eater, feeling that for once in my life I was in the presence of what Rabelais would have called a Gastrolater; insensitive to the elements, unthinking of ordinary human misery, uncaring of the final end to such appetite, she was wrapped in a worship of her belly. "Yes," she said simply and sat back for her priest to attend her.

I was awed. Naïve as I was then in the ways of transatlantic liners, I knew our fare was nothing compared to what was served six or seven decks higher up. I wished with a kind of horror that I would meet this immortal again—in First.

I was to learn, somewhat regretfully, that the more people paid for their fares, the less they ate of the fare's fare and the fewer times they strolled biliously into the luxurious dining room on B-deck to peck at the fantastically generous and rich food provided for their amusement. Instead they paid even more than they would on dry land, once having got onto the most crowded and therefore most desirable ships, for the privilege of avoiding almost all of their fellow passengers by dining in some small and quite often stuffy and viewless restaurant called a club. It was ridiculous, but I must admit it could be fun.

One ship I crossed on several times boasted a tiny room where each day a luncheon was devoted to a country: Monday it would be Sweden, Tuesday China, and so on. I have never since eaten such good national dishes in my life, anywhere. I have never since eaten so much either. The sea change worked its magic, and I sat for three or four hours every midday, savoring everything with a capacity which is unknown to me now, but which in the elegant little dining room had nothing gluttonous about it, nor gross. Smoked eel and aquavit, Hung Yuen Gai Ding and tiger-bone wine—what was in the glasses tipped ever so slightly this way and that, and our hearts felt the tide's pull.

And in the main dining salon dully benighted souls ate their way stodgily, or so we believed in our own tight supercilious little seagoing island, through one endless meal after another, while decks below them still other human beings, less moneyed, less well aired, but in some cases equally blessed by good digestion, had to forego caviar for kippers in what was, even so, a gastronomical spree.

The truth is that no matter what cabin a passenger pays for on a luxury liner, he feels that he has simply bought his passage and is getting his meals free. And when he is confronted with a dinner card as big as the front page of his home-town paper, with no prices visible, he can only treat it according to his lights—his liver and lights, to make a carnal and abattoirish pun.

Perhaps he has known slow true hunger. Then he does one of two things: he either shudders away from such a vulgar show and asks for dry toast and tea, or he does in his own limited way what my Gargantuan fellow passenger did on the *Berengaria*— he eats imperturbably from the "free" Radis et Céleris Frais to the "free" Café Turque. If he is somewhat further removed from the pangs and passions of his belly, by politics or the stock market or even marriage, he becomes more exacting.

And now I think of one of the worst times I ever had on a ship, when I was finagled into introducing a Very Rich Passenger to my friends the Purser and Master Chef, and then was invited to a few exquisite little dinners with this Very Rich Passenger, arranged of course with great to-do by the Purser himself and the Master Chef himself, the kind of dinners for which, almost literally, one bird was stuffed inside another and another and roasted and then we ate the innermost truffle-stuffed olives, with my two friends beaming and gleaming proudly; and then at the last I had to listen to the miserable story of how the Very Rich Passenger skipped ship, on the harbor tender, and did not pay a single tip. I wanted to evaporate with embarrassment, since I am a firm believer in friendship and in tipping, and I am a practitioner of both. I still dread meeting my two friends again.

I comfort myself with the thought of countless other people who have gone back and forth on ocean liners, reveling with far from innocent pleasure in the somewhat decadent excesses of the transatlantic fare, and paying proper fees for those excesses to the servitors who made them possible.

I see them emerging from bedrooms lined with rare woods and heavy with the scent of jungle flowers, in fair gowns and knife-sharp creases, only a little tipsy-crazy from the sea's roll and that last cocktail. I see them happily wandering the length of long buffets set with tubs of caviar in snow, and thick yellow casseroles of truffleblack pâté from Strasbourg. I see them ordering from a hundred knowingly selected ocean-going wines.

It is a shame that I must confess I seldom figured in this pretty picture: early in my travelings I found that for my own peace of mind I must shun most of my fellow passengers. I could not cope with their behavior, there at sea level where so many social inhibitions went overboard, with the protocol of stuffiness on one hand, the licentious whoring on the other.

I worked out my own pattern, dictated by my glandular condition of the moment, and it was something like this when in 1940 I ceased for a time my interurban voyages:

I slept and read, rolling like a delicately balanced log with the ship, until noon. Then after various sybaritic dabblings I went to the bar, not the main one but a tiny place familiar with leather chairs and peanuts in bowls and a discreetly gossipy man named some variation of Fritz who poured fine beer or made impeccable Martinis. I took beer, and I could have been in the Lausanne-Palace, or the Ritz, or . . . or. . . . There was dignity about the very banality of the place. I sensed it and sat back, watching Fritz's ears prick to gossip and his busy eyes flicker cynically over the sleep-fattened faces in front of him.

Then I went to lunch, not in the dining salon but in a little restaurant where I had engaged my table before the ship sailed. I ate and drank and ate and drank, and in a drugged way it was fun.

I always skipped tea, just as I skipped breakfast and the midmorning consommé and crackers, even though tea had a ghoulishly interesting "concert" with it, at which the captain now and then tangoed carefully with one of the three richest women present, and then, even more carefully, with the current femme fatale. I hated teas, tangos, and in a lesser way the lethal women, and went instead to the movies, where I lazily watched ten-year-old-and-tomorrow's cinema seductions and sipped a mild Pernod with water.

The ritual of "dressing" is a pleasure so removed from the present that I look back on it with much the same helpless emotion that I feel about a ten-pound tin of caviar a friend brought me to Dijon from Moscow in 1931: I can only dream of its present impossibility, as I do of the hot water and the countless towels and the dreamy leisure.

Before dinner, ordered in advance from a sheet which had nothing to do with the vulgar printed menu of the main dining salon, I drank either champagne or two very dry Martinis, depending on whether the captain's chart marked the wind velocity at 3 or 7. The little bar (I *never* went into the main bar!) was full and amusing.

Dinner in the club, which suddenly might sprout orchids on its walls or pine branches from the Black Forest behind which tired, invisible cabin boys tootled bird whistles, dinner was indeed exquisite.

And then, after dancing perhaps, or talking in the bar, *my* bar, came the best part of the pattern, when I went to my cabin and there, in the soft light by my bed, was the same curiously exciting and satisfying thing each night: a split of my favorite champagne in a little silver bucket, and a silver plate of the thinnest sandwiches in the world, made knowingly of unbuttered fine bread, slivered breast of chicken, and a generous amount of cayenne pepper. I really do not understand what chord it was in my nature that always vibrated at this sight, but hum and twang it did, inevitably, and still does, in my mind.

I forget what it used to cost, in those happily vanished days, to lunch and loll and sup thus fatuously, but it was one-tenth of what it cost the steamship company to put on such a rich-bitch show—one-tenth or one-fiftieth. And I wonder now what it would cost to make me young enough again to love it, and all the silken extravagance it meant. I think back on it with no regret, but still with a real nostalgia.

And in some ways also I would like to be a lithe, eager twenty and sit across from an immortal big-bosomed implacable Gastrolater who could say "Yes!" and mean it.

I would, but less so, like to be a suave thirty—the caviar was so good then and so plentiful, and I do so love caviar.

Nostalgia hits all my five senses, and colors and perfumes my thoughts. Still I remain upright and cogent, in the face of such a backlog of remembrance, knowing that I, like many another honest gastronomer, can safely lean in secret, now and then, on such things as the word nautical.

I

There is for me a special lure in the names of English puddings: the Steamed Spotted Dog my Aunt Gwen used to make for our delectation, and the Chocolate Mud. They have a realistic ugliness about them which sums up my whole finicky adult approach to something inseparable from the unquestioning, lusty appetite of childhood.

When I was little I was happy in the presence of unlimited Treacle Sponge. Now I would pull away from it and agree with the old proverb, "Cold pudding settles one's love"—right to the pit of one's stomach, I could add.

My interest in even the most bluntly named sweets is largely clinical by now. I can produce one when visiting adolescent nephews make it seem advisable, something like a rich caramel mousse piled with whipped cream and shaved toasted almonds(!), which vanishes almost before it has been set upon the table. I can taste and admire some such daintier masterpiece as was made for me lately in a San Francisco restaurant, a poached fresh peach in chilled zabaglione, very delicate and, as far as any dessert can be, refreshing. (Another one, just as pretty to the eye, was beyond my capacity even to admire after a long winy dinner: a cœur à la crème aux fraises.)

I continue to be baffled by such gastronomical somersaults, but I must acknowledge their necessity to many finer palates than my own, and can even serve forth, here on the page, two of my favorite infallibles, as English as Suet Mould.

North Country Tart

short pastry	*sugar*
gooseberries, or any fruit in season	*thick cream*

Line a deep baking dish with the pastry and cover with fruit and ample sugar. Put in a layer of the pastry that is a little smaller than the dish, then more fruit and sugar. Repeat this. Then cover the dish with a top layer of pastry, pinch it well around the top, cut a little hole in the center, and bake in a hot oven for about 45 minutes. The fruit and sugar will make a fine rich syrup for the two floating layers of pastry. Serve hot in the winter, cold in the summer, and always with a jug of thick chilled cream.

This is a really heavenly sweet, as even I will swear to. It should obviously come at the end of a simple and not too heavy family supper rather than a proper party dinner, but I have occasionally used it as a kind of titillation, a gastronomical gambit, in an otherwise more sophisticated menu.

A suaver pudding, still very, very British indeed, is my version of a recipe served at the famous Hind's Head, which I have found versatile and apparently pleasing to less limited palates than mine. It seems more like a tart than a pudding to my American mind, just as the North Country Tart is more like a pie or a pudding.

Duke of Cambridge Pudding

short pastry	6 *tablespoons butter*
1 *cup chopped candied or*	6 *tablespoons sugar*
heavily preserved fruits	2 *or 3 egg yolks, depending on*
brandy, enough to moisten	*size*
fruit (kirsch is good with	
cherries)	

Line 9-inch baking plate (pie pan!) with crust, making a good, firm, pinched rim. Soak fruit in liquor about an hour, so as to be soft but not mushy. Melt butter in double boiler; add sugar, mix well, stir in egg yolks, and stir gently until thickened. Lightly drain fruit, spread over crust, and pour the cream over it. Bake in hot (425°) oven until the top browns and crinkles. Serve hot or cold.

Of course nothing could ever be quite as good as Aunt Gwen's Muds and Sponges, but as I look back over the spiritual recording of these English sweets, I suddenly feel that perhaps the best one I ever ate, which served as a kind of psychological bridge, was at Simpson's on the Strand, in 1935 or '36. It came as the summation of all such puddings and led me gracefully from childhood hunger to maturity. It came in the springtime after a long, dour London winter, the kind in which I was photographed on Easter Sunday, without my knowing, battling my way across Hyde Park in a whirl of enormous snowflakes. "Visiting Yankee Feels at Home in Unseasonable Blizzard" was one of the newspaper captions. And lunch at Simpson's was a daily ritual, a kind of amiable stoking of my overworked human furnace.

I ate happily through a monumental cut off the joint, with its accompanying "two vegs.," and then a "winter salad," composed largely of pickled beets as I remember, and then, ah, then, came the plum tart, hot, bathed in a flood of Cornish cream, steaming and flowing in the ample plate! How rich it was, how sweet and revivifying to my cold and enervated and above all *young* body! How its steam and savor engulfed and comforted me!

Yes, that was the best pudding of my whole pudding life, and Aunt Gwen would understand my betrayal of all others for it, even her Christmas Bun, when we could play Snap around it with raisins burning in the holiday bath of rum.

O *is for*
Ostentation

. . . and how dignity is most often lacking in it but need not be, at table or anywhere.

While it is very true that rich Amphitryons (and that is indeed an ostentatious way of saying hosts!) are more apt to strut and attempt bedazzlement than poor ones, I think it quite possible for a bowl of soup and a crust of bread to be served with the pompous affectation that in any social milieu spells real ostentation.

In a subtle reversing of the law, it is a poor man who might most easily be ostentatious if he pretended riches and served forth a truffled turkey rather than a stew, to impress me for no matter what venal reason; but a rich man who with great show invited me to sup on pottage would be equally suspect. In either case my gastronomical suspicions, dormant somewhere between my heart and my stomach, would be roused to the lasting damage of my innocent appetite. Why, I would ask, is the stage thus set for me? Why has the delicate peace of a friendly table been thus threatened?

More often than not, ostentatious dining has little dignity

about it, although the combination is possible. I can think of one good literary proof of this apparent contradiction: the unforgettable dinner in *Alice Adams* by Booth Tarkington. That Mrs. Adams served wilted canapés of caviar, without cocktails in that Prohibition day and without even warning her husband what to call them, could be a perfect example of undignified ostentation if it were not for her true nobility, her enormous generosity in wishing, by this puny attempt at worldliness, to work a miracle for her daughter. She failed, in a masterpiece of misery-at-table, but her innate goodness kept her effort from vulgarity.

The other side of the medal, to my mind, is the supper that the two protagonists in *Hotel Imperial* by Arnold Bennett ate in an oyster bar in London: one of the richest girls in the world and the manager of one of her world's most luxurious hotels. Their enjoyment of simplicity, while artfully told as if with sympathy, is a good example of gastronomical pomposity. They are slumming. They are carried away by their own God-like sharing of food with mortal men. They are being infinitely more undignified than if they had walked out in a huff because the oyster bar did not carry the brand of caviar their hotel could produce so easily and quickly.

A queen can, if she indeed be queenly, serve forth a ghastly meal with as much dignity as Mrs. Adams. If I were Disraeli, for instance (one of the few people I would not mind having been, although if I had been he I would most probably have minded the being, a fine but obvious distinction), I would think nothing of a dinner with Her Majesty Victoria something on this order, as served, say, in the summer of 1841 by her dashing Chief Cook and Maître d'Hôtel Francatelli.

There were two services—the first consisted of four soups; four fish dishes; four different hors d'œuvres of lobster claws; four "removes" (truffled pullets, ham in aspic, stuffed leg of lamb, beef fillets larded with anchovies); sixteen entrées ranging from turtle fins with a Madeira sauce through roasted pigeon breasts; and a "sideboard" of venison, roast beef, roast mutton, and what was in 1841 called "vegetables," an overcooked, overseasoned, and usually ignored collection of turnips, potatoes, and Brussels sprouts.

The second service, after a recess which with the Queen present was apt to be more bluntly digestive than wittily revivifying, began with six roasts—two each of quail, young hares, and chickens. Then came six different kinds of puddings, a strange remnant of Elizabethan days when baked honeyed dishes made in part of eggs were as liable to be based on cabbage as on vanilla cream. Two main edible ornaments and four minor ones accompanied these horrendous sweets: they were monumental, minareted, and buttressed with a thousand elaborate swirls of nougat, caramel, and almond paste, and they were, from the evidence of Victorian menu cards, a variation of the sixteenth-century "set piece" essential to any honest-to-God dinner party.

Next, and finally, came sixteen side dishes, or entremets, which in another fifty years or so were to turn into the present British idea (or better, dream) of a savory. Today that means, at least in memory, a small, would-be appetizing and usually hot nibble of highly seasoned cheese and/or fish and/or pâté (a classic example is John Fothergill's recipe for Little Cat, which includes grated cheese, anchovy or curry, cayenne pepper, scraped onion, chutney). When Disraeli was dining, more or less at the helm of state, the future savory included a kind of reverse Russian-buffet of everything from truffles to gooseberry jelly, a macédoine of fresh fruits, new green peas à la française, string beans in butter, strawberry tarts, artichokes, a chicken aspic, whipped cream with sugared almonds. An incredible hodgepodge!

Disraeli, like most of the other familiars at the Queen's board, thought little of this meal, if anything. He chose what he wanted, sent away what did not please him, asked for and was poured the drinks he fancied, in an elegant confusion which was routine, scheduled, and even mildly enjoyable. And there at Buckingham it was removed from any slightest hint of undignified ostentation, either gastronomical or social.

Anywhere else? No matter how wealthy a brewer or duke or shipbuilder might find himself in that time of rolling Victorian riches when many a merchant prince could have bought out the Crown, he would have been damned indeed if he had tried to imitate this royal show. Anywhere else it would have been too smug, too long, above all too undignified, for even Disraeli to choke down.

The Queen's fantastic dinners, like poor Mrs. Adams' heat-wracked party for her daughter, had a rhythm of nobility about them; they were unconscious of such nonsense as the capacity of the human belly or the perquisites of local custom. If the Queen or Mrs. Adams had known better, and had still put on their shows for reasons of low cunning known as state, Disraeli (and I) would have spat out the nourishment rather than be sickened by the lies. As it was, the countless dishes of the one and the sad little curling canapés of the other had the same regal disregard of men, weather, and history, while any such self-conscious little feast as the one eaten in a London oyster bar by two refugees from velvet has an uncomfortable condescension about it.

Few of us can honestly admit that at some time in our lives we have not swanked, gastronomically: at school, when we pretended cookies made by our mother and sent in the weekly laundry box were really baked by a nonexistent cook (or vice versa and just as ostentatiously); in business, when we have ordered truffled quail at Romanoff's instead of a Number Nine at Lindy's to please a possible client (or vice versa!); in love, most

of all perhaps, when we have put on a painful show of utter so-
phistication or of complete simplicity in order to win a sexual
prize who, if worth its basic ration of good honest salt, would
recognize such flummery and cast it out.

All of that is ostentation, familiar to the human animal. It
need not be expensive, although usually it is: a show of opulence
has always been fashionable, but a gutter rat can be ostentatious
if necessary, in his own way, with the butt-end of a dead cigar.
In other words, it is relative and as varied as the men who practice it. The one thing it most often lacks, although that too can
be a part of it, is the one thing that can redeem it: at least a modicum of unself-conscious dignity.

I

A recipe from an unidentifiable cookery book published in
London in 1814, dedicated to a duke as they all had to be, gives
a formula that makes a pretty contrast to what I myself do to
fresh zucchini, the nearest decent gastronomical counterpart to
those overgrown pithy garden monsters called vegetable mar-
rows in England:

Vegetable-Marrow à la Poulette

*Cut the legumes, according to their size and age, into sections of four,
six, or eight, like oranges; peel them thoroughly, trim them neatly, and
put them into a basin with ample salt and vinegar, and steep for several
hours. Pour off the resultant liquid, and put them into a deep sautapan
thickly spread with butter, and season well with nutmeg, mignonette-
pepper, salt, and a large spoon of powdered sugar. Moisten with half a
pint of white broth, and set to boil gently over a stove-fire until they become quite tender; this will require a half-hour or an hour. Then boil
them down in their glaze; it must then be poured off, and a gravy-spoon
of* Velouté *added; finish by simmering the vegetable-marrows over the
lively fire for a few minutes, and incorporating with them a leason of*

four yolks of eggs, mixed with half a gill of cream, a spoonful of chopped and boiled parsley, and the juice of half a lemon; dish them up with a border of short fleurons *and serve.*

This in its own fantastic pre-Victorian way is a kind of frittata. Today's pressure-cooking takes the place in a few seconds of the hours of soaking and simmering the old cooks needed, or so they thought, to make a vegetable soft enough, and enough drained of its own forthright flavor and worth, to set before a duke.

When I can buy zucchini not over four inches long and preferably with the little withered blossom still clinging to the umbilicus, I lightly brush them under cold water, cut off both ends, and cook them for something less than two minutes in my Presto. I drain them at once, saving the fine green juice for everything from midmorning broth to borscht, and then what I can salvage from my children's avid fingers I sprinkle with grated Parmesan, and bake whole and quickly, five minutes or so in a hot oven in a buttered casserole, and serve forth, unadorned by nutmeg or powdered sugar or even salt and pepper! They are sweet, somehow nutlike, infinitely fresh.

And now and then I make a frittata, an honest, delicate concoction, which will be honestly but very indelicately loathed by anyone honest enough to confess to a basic loathing for zucchini (it can be made with any fresh cooked vegetable, such as green beans).

Frittata alla Anything-at-All

½ cube butter (4 or 5 tablespoons)	1 to 2 cups freshly cooked vegetables in small pieces (zucchini, eggplant, cauliflower, plain or mixed)
1 green pepper, coarsely chopped	
3 tablespoons chopped parsley	

2 tablespoons minced shallots,
    scallions, or chives, or/and
    herbs
6 to 8 eggs

1 cup good cream
4 to 6 tablespoons grated
    Parmesan
salt, fresh grated pepper

Brown butter in casserole in hot (450°) oven. Add green pepper, onion, and herbs and mix well. Reduce oven heat to about 350° and let mixture get partly cooked. Add cooked vegetables, mix well, and let reach bubbling point. Stir (do not beat) eggs gently with cream, cheese, and seasoning, and pour into the very hot casserole. Turn off oven, return casserole to it, and bake the mixture slowly in the heat, taking care that it does not bubble and pulling it away once or twice with a fork from the sides to the center of the dish. Serve as soon as fairly firm in center; otherwise it will be overdone by the time it reaches the table. For a more pungent frittata use olive oil rather than butter and increase the herbs and ingredients according to taste—garlic, anchovy fillets, that sort of thing.

P *is for* Peas

. . . naturally! and for a few reasons why the best peas I ever ate in my life were, in truth, the best peas I ever ate in my life.

Every good cook, from Fanny Farmer to Escoffier, agrees on three things about these delicate messengers to our palates from the kind earth mother: they must be very green, they must be freshly gathered, and they must be shelled at the very last second of the very last minute.

My peas, that is, the ones that reached an almost unbelievable summit of perfection, an occasion that most probably never would happen again, met these three gastronomical requirements to a point of near-ridiculous exactitude. It is possible, however, that even this technical impeccability would not have been enough without the mysterious blending, that one time, of weather, place, other hungers than my own. After all, I can compare bliss with near bliss, for I have often, blessèd me, eaten superlative green peas.

Once, for instance, my grandmother ran out into her garden, filled her apron with the fattest pods, sat rocking jerkily with a kind of nervous merriment for a very few minutes as she shelled them—and before we knew it she had put down upon the white-covered table a round dish of peas in cream. We ate them with our spoons, something we never could have done at home! Perhaps that added to their fragile, poignant flavor, but not much: they were truly *good*.

And then once in Paris, in June (what a hackneyed but wonderful combination of the somewhat overrated time-and-place motif!), I lunched at Foyot's, and in the dim room where hothouse roses stood on all the tables the very month roses climbed crazily outside on every trellis, I watched the headwaiter, as skilled as a magician, dry peas over a flame in a generous pan, add what looked like an equal weight of butter, which almost visibly sent out a cloud of sweet-smelling hay and meadow air, and then swirl the whole.

At the end he did a showy trick, more to amuse himself than me, but I sat openmouthed, and I can still see the arc of little green vegetables flow up into the air and then fall, with a satisfying shush, back into the pan some three or four feet below and at least a yard from where they took off. I gasped, the headwaiter bowed faintly but with pride, and then we went about the comparatively mundane procedure of serving, tasting, and eating.

Those petits pois au beurre were, like my grandmother's, à la crème mode d'Iowa, good—*very* good. They made me think of paraphrasing Sidney Smith's remark about strawberries and saying, "Doubtless God could have made a better green pea, but doubtless He never did."

That was, however, before the year I started out, on a spring date set by strict local custom, to grow peas in a steep terraced garden among the vineyards between Montreux and Lausanne, on the Lake of Geneva.

The weather seemed perfect for planting by May Day, and I had the earth ready, the dry peas ready, the poles ready to set up. But Otto and Jules, my mentors, said no so sternly that I promised to wait until May 15, which could easily be labeled Pea-

Planting Day in Swiss almanacs. They were right, of course: we had a cold snap that would have blackened any sprout about May 10. As I remember, the moon, its rising, and a dash of hailstones came into the picture too.

And then on May 15, a balmy sweet day if ever I saw one, my seeds went into the warm, welcoming earth, and I could agree with an old gardening manual which said understandingly, "Perhaps no vegetable is set out in greater expectancy . . . for the early planting fever is impatient."

A week later I put in another row, and so on for a month, and they did as they were meant to, which is one of the most satisfying things that can possibly happen to a gardener, whether greenhorn and eager or professional and weatherworn.

Then came the day with stars on it: time for what my grandmother would have called "the first mess of peas."

The house at Le Pâquis was still a-building, shapes of rooms but no roof, no windows, trestles everywhere on the wide terrace high above the lake, the ancient apple tree heavily laden with button-sized green fruit, plums coloring on the branches at the far end near the little meadow, set so surprisingly among the vineyards that gave Le Pâquis its name.

We put a clean cloth, red and white, over one of the carpenters' tables, and we kicked wood curls aside to make room for our feet under the chairs brought up from the apartment in Vevey. I set out tumblers, plates, silver, smooth, unironed napkins sweet from the meadow grass where they had dried.

While some of us bent over the dwarf-pea bushes and tossed the crisp pods into baskets, others built a hearth from stones and a couple of roof tiles lying about and made a lively little fire. I had a big kettle with spring water in the bottom of it, just off simmering, and salt and pepper and a pat of fine butter to hand. Then I put the bottles of Dézelay in the fountain, under the timeless spurt of icy mountain water, and ran down to be the liaison between the harvesters and my mother, who sat shelling peas from the basket on her lap into the pot between her feet, her fingers as intent and nimble as a lacemaker's.

I dashed up and down the steep terraces with the baskets, and my mother would groan and then hum happily when another one appeared, and below I could hear my father and our friends cursing just as happily at their wry backs and their aching thighs, while the peas came off their stems and into the baskets with a small sound audible in that still high air, so many hundred feet above the distant and completely silent Léman. It was suddenly almost twilight. The last sunlight on the Dents du Midi was fire-rosy, with immeasurable coldness in it.

"Time, gentlemen, time," my mother called in an unrehearsed and astonishing imitation of a Cornish barmaid.

They came in grateful hurry up the steep paths, almost nothing now in their baskets, and looks of smug success upon their faces. We raced through the rest of the shelling, and then while we ate rolled prosciutto and drank Swiss bitters or brandy and soda or sherry, according to our various habits, I dashed like an eighteenth-century courier on a secret mission of utmost military importance, the pot cautiously braced in front of me, to the little hearth.

I stirred up the fire. When the scant half-inch of water boiled, I tossed in the peas, a good six quarts or more, and slapped on the heavy lid as if a devil might get out. The minute steam showed I shook the whole like mad. Someone brought me a curl of thin pink ham and a glass of wine cold from the fountain. Revivified, if that were any more possible, I shook the pot again.

I looked up at the terrace, a shambles of sawed beams, cement mixers, and empty sardine tins left from the workmen's lunches. There sat most of the people in the world I loved, in a thin light that was pink with Alpen glow, blue with a veil of pine smoke from the hearth. Their voices sang with a certain remoteness into the clear air, and suddenly from across the curve of the Lower Corniche a cow in Monsieur Rogivue's orchard moved her head among the meadow flowers and shook her bell in a slow, melodious rhythm, a kind of hymn. My father lifted up his face at the sweet sound and, his fists all stained with green-pea juice, said passionately, "God, but I feel good!" I felt near to tears.

The peas were now done. After one more shake I whipped off the lid and threw in the big pat of butter, which had a bas-relief of William Tell upon it. I shook in salt, ground in pepper, and then swirled the pot over the low flames until Tell had disappeared. Then I ran like hell, up the path lined with candytuft and pinks, past the fountain where bottles shone promisingly through the crystal water, to the table.

Small brown roasted chickens lay on every plate, the best ones I have ever eaten, done for me that afternoon by Madam Doellenbach of the Vieux Vevey and not chilled since but cooled in their own intangibly delicate juices. There was a salad of mountain lettuces. There was honest bread. There was plenty of limpid wine, the kind Brillat-Savarin said was like rock-water, tempting enough to make a hydrophobic drink. Later there was cheese, an Emmenthaler and a smuggled Roblichon . . .

. . . And later still we walked dreamily away, along the Upper Corniche to a café terrace, where we sat watching fireworks far across the lake at Evian, and drinking café noir and a very fine *fine*.

But what really mattered, what piped the high unforgettable tune of perfection, were the peas, which came from their hot pot onto our thick china plates in a cloud, a kind of miasma, of everything that anyone could ever want from them, even in a dream. I recalled the three basic requisites, according to Fanny

Farmer and Escoffier . . . and again I recalled Sidney Smith, who once said that his idea of Heaven (and he was a cleric!) was pâté de foie gras[1] to the sound of trumpets. Mine, that night and this night too, is fresh green garden peas, picked and shelled by my friends, to the sound of a cowbell.

I

Conveniently, P is for pâté as well as peas, and I continue to feel near enough to Sidney Smith, my long-time ideal of a charming person, to agree with him that the former can be as heavenly as the latter, with or without the sound of trumpets!

I used to think, and perhaps still do, that I can never really have enough pâté de foie gras. I spent almost a half a year in Strasbourg once and could eat it at will, or at least whenever I could justify splurging from twenty to forty American cents for a generous slice of it, which seemed to be more often than not.

There was a "patriotic" *brasserie*, reputedly run by the French government at a hideous financial loss in order to indoctrinate Gallic gaiety into the morbid confused basically Germanic citizens, and there we could eat delicious, well-served pâté in aspic for six francs, as I remember, which would rightly have cost three times as much in any café less bent toward propaganda.

Once in a while we went to a very pompous, small, elegant restaurant, Prussian as a slashed cheek, and ordered pâté de foie gras truffé en brioche, a culinary trick that has always fascinated me, like the Baked Alaska of my adolescence. How does the rich goose liver stay whole and fresh while the dough bakes? And how did the ice cream stay cold and firm while the magic white mound of meringue turned gold? (I prefer to remain puzzled over the former, and leave the latter to my wide-eyed children.)

I used to go, now and then in Strasbourg, to the Doyen offices and choose little or big pots, according to my purse, to be sent back to America. The eighteenth-century Doyen, the founder, is said to be the man who first put truffles into his paste of fat goose livers and spice and brandy, and he or whoever else it may have been who consummated this celestial wedding of high flavor should be tendered some special gastronomical salute, it seems to me, just as should the brave soul who first ate a tomato, and the equally hardy one who first evolved a Camembert cheese from a fermenting pudding of old cream. There is nothing much better in this Western world than a fine, unctuous, truffled pâté, and I suspect that when next I taste one, packed and shipped from Strasbourg itself, I shall be hard put to it not to shed a tear of impious nostalgic bliss upon it.

Meanwhile I look back with no great difficulty to many a pâté maison I have enjoyed, most of which had never even seen the shadow of a fat goose liver. They were delicious.

In general, from Paris to New York, the smaller the maison of which it was the pâté, the better it tasted: an inverse attempt to be important, I suppose, made the little restaurants exert themselves to produce an honorable substitute for the real thing, while the big ones simply took it for granted that anyone who could afford them would of course order nothing but genuine pâté de foie gras de Strasbourg.

Whatever the materialistic reasons for this triumph, I have eaten many unheralded pâtés that almost, if not quite, comforted me for the unavoidable realization that they were but substitutes. I have often made them myself, not always with as good fortune as some of the professional chefs whose loaves I have cut into, but still passing well—passing damn well. I have found that it takes time to make them properly, that they improve with aging, that they must hold only the best of whatever ingredients they call for (no cheap butter, for instance, no "cooking" brandy), and that they must be quietly but sternly heady with the fumes of freshly ground pepper, fine smoky bacon fat, sweet butter, honest booze. If properly served, cold and smooth from their casseroles or terrines, with good crusty bread and good red wine, they need touch the lock to none.

The best of these pâtés that I have ever tasted, but not made myself, was one sent to a friend in Dijon from Brillat-Savarin's town of Belley, and kept on a ledge in the wine cellar all summer. Then, one of the first nippy days of fall, Monsieur Ollagnier lifted it down from its cobwebs. While we all leaned, noses to windward, over the table, he broke open the hard flour crust that was the seal. He lifted it off delicately, in one fine piece, mildewed on top and closed impregnably, underneath, with yellow, cold, chaste fat. He plunged his knife sharply, surely, into one end of the casserole.

Madame Ollagnier clashed the plates roughly toward him, as if afraid to lose one crumb upon the cloth, and their son stood up pontifically, for nineteen that is, and prepared to pour the Nuit-St.-Georges Grands Suchots, with which we planned to drink to countless unpresent souls.

The pâté itself was truly a hunters' dish, worthy of Belley and its mighty ghost, a heady, gamy mixture, laced as tight as an 1880 belle with the best local brandy, high as a kite with spices and forest herbs, a true pâté de gibier à la mode de whoever made it, like this one of mine:

Pâté Fin
(pour Fêtes)

1 hare (or equivalent bulk of quail, pheasant, duck, what you will), the best parts	1 pound good meat from hare or whatever meat is being used (scraps)
equal weight of lean bacon in thin strips	6 ounces pork
	6 ounces veal
	1 pound bacon

3 or 4 *thinly sliced truffles, if possible*	1 *egg*
brandy	1 *scant cup brandy*
	bay, nutmeg, etc., as desired

Bone the best parts of the hare (assuming you are making a pâté de lièvre), and put them with an equal weight of bacon and the sliced truffles into a casserole. Marinate in brandy to cover.

Make a forcemeat of the clean scrapmeat, pork, veal, and bacon, and run through a fine meat grinder twice. Mix well with the egg and brandy and put through a fine sieve.

Line an oval or round terrine carefully with the marinated bacon strips, and then fill it with alternating layers of hare, forcemeat, and bacon, scattering the precious truffles judiciously. Cover with bacon. Put on bay, etc., as desired. Cover with a heavy lid, set in a pan of water, and bake in a slow (325°) oven. When the ample grease that rises to the top is quite clear, the pâté is done, and not before.

Remove from oven, cool, and then let chill at least two days before serving. If care is taken to use only the best ingredients, and to see that the top "butter" is absolutely clear before removing from the stove, this pâté will last in a cold place for many months, and it will be worth the guarding of it.

I would, if I could, send a pot of it, in Heaven surely, to Sidney Smith himself.

Q is for
Quantity

. . . and for The Case of the Hindu Eggs, as well as the case of some people, many of them gastronomical as well as human, who honestly believe that if a recipe calls for two cups of butter it will be twice as good if they use four.

If Escoffier, or Mrs. Mazza, or Henry Low, asks for one teaspoon of béchamel, one teaspoon of chopped basil, or one teaspoon of soy sauce, these mistaken searchers for the jewel of perfection will double the dose, and in so doing wreck themselves. The ones who thus continue assaulting the palates of their intimates deserve rather than mercy a good stiff lecture on the pleasures of the table as opposed to the wounds of an outraged tongue, and if that fails they should be, quite bluntly, crossed off the gastronomical list.

There is no hope for a cook who will not learn his own as well as other gourmets' limitations, and a man who has made one good béchamel by rote, one good minestrone, or one good Yat Gai Mein, and then goes on to make impossible ones because of his lack of balance, perspective, and plain common sense and modesty, is, to be blunt again, past recall.

Of course it must be added here that many a clumsy amateur who early believed in all good faith that enough of a good thing could never be too much has later turned into a chef of subtlety and breeding, just as many a man who later learned to judge the points of a setter picked out, in his first dog-days, his own early puppyhood, a male because he was big, or a bitch for her pretty eyes. It takes some people a long time to realize that there are rules which have filtered into our life-patterns in a near perfect state, just as it takes other people to act as a kind of ferment, forever questioning these rules or others like them, in rich rebellion.

Gastronomical precepts are perhaps among the most delicate ones in the modern arts. They must, in the main, be followed before they can be broken: that is, I can do something with five given ingredients that Escoffier perhaps never dreamed of, but in order to do it well I must follow his basic rules for white stock, glaze, and poaching, which he and all his kind perfected in a grueling devotion to their métier.

A rebuttal to this hidebound theory could be that gastronomical accidents often give birth to beauty: a chef forgets the fried potatoes, pops them out and then into the fat, and has pommes soufflées; another cook adds a raw yolk quickly to a portion of scrambled eggs when he finds it is to serve two people instead of one and has a new nutlike flavor on his conscience and his reputation. There are uncountable anecdotes of such chance discoveries.[1] Basically they have nothing to do with the fact that certain rules must be followed in order to reach certain results, in the sublime chemistry of food. They must, as Brillat-Savarin pointed out in his quasi-solemn little lecture on the art of frying, spring from a knowledge of natural laws.

My own rude forcing in the school of obedience to them came, perhaps fortunately for myself and certainly with great good luck for my intimates, when I was about nine.

I had already learned to follow recipes and could, I say now with a somewhat smug astonishment, make pan gravy, blanc-mange (cornstarch pudding), jelly roll, and other like requisites for my maternal grandmother's diet, and a few stolen delicacies such as mayonnaise, which we ate hungrily when she went away to religious conventions. I felt at home in the kitchen, at least on the cook's day off, and could poach eggs with the best of them, standing tiptoe on a needlepoint footstool beside the gas range.

But there was, as always, a salutary comeuppance. It happened one time when my father and mother went away for a Sunday and I was appointed to make a nice little supper for my sister and myself. I read a recipe in one of the smudged kitchen standbys. Hindu Eggs,[2] it said, and it was not the exotic title but the fact that curry powder was among the ingredients that decided me. The procedure was simple, quite within my skills, and as I boiled eggs and made a cream sauce I thought happily of that half-teaspoonful of curry, and of all the other delicious curried dishes of lamb and suchlike that we had sneaked when Grandmother was, as she was that very day, in Long Beach or Asbury Park.

The eggs peeled miraculously smooth. The sauce was a bland velvet dream. The casserole was buttered. And then I chose destruction: in a voluptuous maze of wanting to see again upon my sister's face the pleasure she always showed when we sneaked a curry, and in my own sensual need for more spice, more excitement, than Grandmother would allow us in our daily food, I put in several tablespoons of the nice yellowish-brownish powder.

The rest of the story is plain to any cook, no matter how amateur, but it conditioned at least two potential gastronomers to look up and murmur "Hindu Eggs!" whenever ignorance or stupidity shows in the seasoning of a dish.

It is fortunate that an obedience to the laws of nature is quite often an inherent thing in a good cook. I know at least one, a woman, who could not possibly say why she adds ice water rather than tap water to her superlative pastry; she can neither read nor write, and indeed can hardly talk, and if she is asked she will say grudgingly, "Kinda makes it set right." She knows what all good cooks do, but not why.

Anyone, though, who wants to make pastry, or any other perquisite of gourmandism, can comfort himself with the certainty that if he is not born with this inarticulate knowledge he can acquire it. He can read, try, observe, think. He can, after a period of trial and inevitable error, somewhat like beginning to skate, turn out a pie as good as my friend's—maybe better. He may be like another chef I know, a dentist, who for his own amusement has translated every one of his heavenly recipes into purely chemical terms and formulas, an occupational whimsy far beyond most people; or he may be content, as am I, to leave "1 c. milk, 3 t. flour," and so on. But if he is honest, he will not tamper with any of the basic rules.

Myself, I have read so many recipes in the past thirty years or so, for both love and hunger, that I can and mostly do separate the good ones from the bad at a glance. What is more, I have followed so many of them, both actually and in my culinary brain, that I unconsciously reword and reorganize most of them, and am rebuffed and made suspicious by anything clumsy in them. For instance, I think a good recipe lists its ingredients in the order of their use, and there are a dozen other such rules I like to see followed.

And one thing I do, always and every time, is to wonder about the pepper in a new recipe. Me, I like pepper. Me, I find that every professional rule, say in *The Settlement* or *The Boston*, puts in about one-half what I want. On the other hand, most amateur recipes call for too much. Always and every time, therefore, my pepper-conscious mind (or palate?) questions the seasoning, and with one eye on what I already know about cooking and the other on what I think I know about the people who will eat my food, I alter the indicated proportions—as far as pepper goes, that is.

Much further than that I do not stray, at least in the basic requirements of fat and flour, flour and liquid, liquid and temperature, and so on. I have learned in my own laborious workshop the culinary laws of nature and by now can fairly well adjust them to the stove at my command, the weather and passions at whose command I am.

I know enough, in other words, not to double the lemon juice in a Hollandaise sauce: it will be too sour and it will probably curdle and it will, in short, be a flop. I know it won't help at all to make a custard of whipping cream instead of milk: it will flop. I know a salad won't be twice as good if I put in two tins of anchovy fillets instead of one. It, and the salt-killed lettuce in it, will flop, and dismally.

On the other hand I can, and do, double the butter or chicken fat when I make kasha,[3] and treble the wine in aspic, and cut the cooking time in half for almost any fish—all these are personal tricks which time has verified for my own taste, once I admit, as heaven knows I do, that I must first obey what the great cooks have found out for me.

What Brillat-Savarin said in 1825 about frying is still true, because it is based on nature's laws, and the same holds for a master like Escoffier on sauces and roasting, for any thoughtful cook, derivative or not, who bows to law and does not wildly say "Twice as much butter, or garlic, or zubzubzub, *must* be twice as good . . . If a pinch of nutmeg picks up this dish of spinach, *two* pinches . . ." and so on.

We who must eat such well-meant messes can do no better than refuse them and then beseech all such misguided cooks to stop and consider, to ponder on the reasons as well as the results, and to decide for themselves and also for our stomachs' sakes to follow the rules based on common sense and experience, the rules set down by great chefs, whatever their sex and in whichever of these last two centuries they have worked.

We must hold out the torch to these taste-deafened friends of ours and promise them that they too can throw away a few, if not all, of their gastronomical hearing aids; they too, once they have learned how to walk among the pots and pipkins, can add saffron where Escoffier said thyme, or put kirsch instead of maraschino into a soufflé—once they have rightly learned what saffron tastes like, and what a soufflé is.

I

The following accidental result of a flustered surmise that the juice of a whole lemon must certainly taste much better than the skimpy teaspoonful the recipe demanded is to my mind a typical Bachelor's Delight, the kind that in its originator's hands can become almost a psychological drama of just-so stirring, a soul-tearing ordeal of finickiness, but that in more nonchalant, calloused hands, culinarily speaking, is almost as easy to make as what the *Ladies' Aid Manual* calls "Plain Sauce."

The rule for it, coaxed with some skulduggery from a highly successful Benedict, is truly one of those gastronomical monstrosities, The Happy Accident: it should be nasty, holding so much flour; it should be inedible, especially when served upon its destined breast of chicken with rice, with so much lemon juice in it; it is not a Hollandaise, not a cream sauce, not anything identifiable. But it is good.

Sauce Happy Accident

½ cup sweet butter	salt, white pepper, cayenne
½ cup flour	1 egg yolk
2 cups strong chicken consommé	juice of one lemon

Gently blend butter and flour over boiling water in double boiler. Heat the strained consommé, add slowly, blend, and stir over simmering water for ½ hour. Season to taste. Five minutes before serving stir lemon juice into egg yolk, pass through fine strainer into sauce, and blend carefully.

This should be very good with something like poached fillets of sole or perch, but I have not tried it. I know that it is rather startling and fresh on properly boiled chicken. My one quarrel with it is that it is too sharp for the white wine that I like to accompany such a dish.

2

It may seem strange thus to return to the scene of the crime, but often since that far-off horrible day, that basically *blessed* day, I have made a more knowing version of this dish. Then it was nothing but sliced hard-boiled eggs covered with a rich cream sauce lightly (or so it said in the recipe!) savorous of good curry powder. Here is my mature adaptation of it, pleasant in hot weather, curry's natural climate, with a green salad and some beer.

Hindu Eggs, 1949

12 peeled hard-boiled eggs	1 tablespoon finely minced onion
½ cup mayonnaise	
1 tablespoon curry powder salt, cayenne pepper	1 tablespoon finely chopped parsley
1 tablespoon soy sauce	3 to 4 cups heavy cream sauce

Cut the eggs once lengthwise and then mix their yolks well with all the other ingredients except the cream sauce: that is, make a good recipe for the deviled eggs of any proper picnic, but adding curry powder. Stuff the eggs, put them together in their proper shape, and let stand several hours or overnight, to bring out the heat of the curry. Place in shallow buttered casserole, cover with hot bland sauce, place in a medium oven until almost bubbling, and serve. Use more cream sauce if it is to be served with rice. The eggs should have a strong curry flavor, in contrast to the gentle sauce, so some experimentation with your brand of curry powder is a good idea.

3

The patriotism of gastronomy has always caused emotional havoc, and who can know if my avowal here that I think Russian kasha one of the world's best dishes may not breed trouble for my children? I hope not. My devotion to the food as such is one of animal satisfaction rather than iron-curtained boundaries, and I feel quite safe in saying that as long as I can buy whole, unadulterated buckwheat groats I shall not only do so but shall prepare them in a fashion predominantly Slavic, even though I may stoop for reasons of family security to dubbing it Greek or Latvian (or Japanese?).

Most kosher delicatessens in this country carry one form or another of uncooked kasha. It is increasingly bad, thanks to the wave of precooking and even predigesting that has swept away good packaged cereals in the last few years: it turns into an ugly mush, not fit to soil the pan.

Unless you are sure of your market and your brand, the best thing is to go to a "health food" store ("My God," a friend exclaimed, waiting outside one while I bought raw sugar for the children and eying the rows of natural-remedy cathartics in the window, "my God, I didn't know *everybody* was so constipated!"). Such stores, once you work past the sugarless candies and the sucroseless sugars and such, have very good honest things like stone-ground oatmeal—and kasha. It should be *whole*, unprecooked, unpasteurized, unvitaminized, and so on, and so on.

Once having got it (and it will be worth the fuss), prepare it more or less according to the following recipe, remembering that if you are like me you will agree to most of the additions I shall make later:

Basic Rule for Kasha

2 *cups whole grain buckwheat*	2 *to 4 cups hot water*
1 *large or 2 small eggs*	2 *tablespoons butter or chicken*
½ *teaspoon salt*	*fat*

Put buckwheat in cold, ungreased, heavy skillet. Break in egg and stir until each grain is coated. Heat gently, stirring often, so that the grains become separate, glossy, and pleasantly odorous. Season. When skillet is hot, add water to cover grains and stir in fat. Put on heavy lid and reduce heat to minimum (or cook covered in 350° oven). Steam for ½ hour to 45 minutes, checking now and then and adding water if too dry. Use as you would rice.

Now here is where I branch off, as an old kasha-hound sniffing my way along ruggedly individual trails!

To begin with, I like to use kasha, made my way naturally, as a light stuffing for anything from old hens to wild turkeys: its straightforward flavor is more unexpected than that of the customary (and delicious) wild rice—and much less expensive. I like it as it comes from the pot, hot with butter or sour cream, and it is one of my daughters' favorite meals, cold in a bowl with cream and brown sugar. I like it mixed lightly with hot sliced mushrooms, or under mushrooms in sharply seasoned sour cream. I like it alongside any gamy meat, from venison to sauer-braten, in or near or quite without a sauce. It seems that I like it.

As for my own rich changes to ring: I do more than dry out the groats in the raw egg—I toast them to the nutty stage, very carefully, as if they were almonds. Then, instead of adding water, I use either good meat stock (tinned consommé is good) or vegetable juice from my pressure-cooker stock. I heat this, pour it on carefully so that it does not leap right out again with the heat, put double the advised amount of good butter or chicken fat or goose fat in the middle of the puddle, and batten down the heavy lid. I let it cook at something below a simmer, so that no fine steam is lost. I add more hot liquid if it seems wise, and every time I do this I put another tablespoon or so of butter into the middle and shake the pan gently without stirring it. It is rather like making a risotto.

When the kasha is fairly dry, cooked but not soft, I stir it, taste it, season it mildly with salt, take it off the fire, and leave it un-covered to air for an hour or more. Then I put what I'll need into a well-buttered casserole and put the casserole in the oven, to heat through at about 350°, usually with another dollop of but-ter (once I had some high-flavored drippings from wild pheas-ants I had cooked the week before, a superlative heady flavor, melted through the kasha!).

This is admittedly a blatant example of rich-bitch deviation from a basically "poor" recipe. I know that I could be grateful for a handful of the beneficent grains, boiled in a little water. I know that some day I may want them that way, desperately. But meanwhile I like them in a cloud of added richness and sa-vor and have no shame in saying so. However they may come, they will be good.

R *is for*
Romantic

. . . and for a few of the reasons that gastronomy is and always has been connected with its sister art of love.

Or perhaps instead of reasons, which everyone who understands anything about digestion and its good and bad endocrinological effects will already know, I should discuss here, with brief discretion, a few direct results of the play of the five senses, properly stimulated by food upon human passion. The surest way, if not the best, is to look backward.

Passion, here at least, means the height of emotional play between the two sexes, not the lasting fire I felt for my father once when I was about seven and we ate peach pie together under a canyon oak, and not the equally lasting fire I felt for a mammoth woman who brought milk toast to me once in the dusk when I was seventeen and very sick, and not the almost searing gratitude I felt for my mother when she soothed me with buttered carrots and a secret piece of divinity fudge once when I had done wrong and was in Coventry, and not the high note of confidence between two human beings that I felt once on a frozen hillside in France when a bitter old general broke his bread in two and gave me half.

This other kind of passion that I speak of, romantic if ever any such brutal thing could be so deemed, is one of sex, of the come-and-go, the preening and the prancing, and the final triumph or defeat, of two people who know enough, subconsciously or not, to woo with food as well as flattery.

The first time I remember recognizing the new weapon I was about eight, I think. There was a boy named Red, immortal on all my spiritual calendars, a tall, scoffing, sneering, dashing fellow perhaps six months older than I, a fellow of withdrawals, mockery, and pain. I mocked back at him, inadequately, filled with a curious tremor.

He followed me home every afternoon from school, a good half-block behind, and over the giggles of my retinue of girl friends came his insults and his lewd asides to a train of knee-britched sycophants. We must have looked very strange to the relics of the Quaker settlers of our little town, who pulled aside their parlor curtains at our noise, but if our pipings were audible to their ancient ears they would not have felt too shocked, for as I recall it all we said, in a thousand significantly differing tones, was, Oh, yeah? Huh! Oh, *yeah?*

My friends gave me advice, as doubtless Red's gave him, and our daily march continued until February 14 that year without much variation. Then Red presented me with the biggest, fanciest, and most expensive Valentine in the class box: we knew, because it still said "50¢" on the back, in a spidery whisper of extravagance marked down thoughtfully in indelible pencil by the bookstore man and left carefully unsmeared by my canny lover.

I stalked on sneeringly every afternoon, virginal amid my train of damsels, the knights behind, hawking and nudging.

I was won, though, being but human and having, at eight as

now, a belly below my heart. Red, through what advice I can never know, a few days later slipped into my desk the first nickel candy bar I had ever seen, called, I think, a Cherriswete.

It was a clumsy lump of very good chocolate and fondant, with a preserved cherry in the middle, all wrapped up in a piece of paper that immediately on being touched sent off waves of red and gilt stain. It was, to me, not only the ultimate expression of masculine devotion, but pure gastronomical delight, in a household where Grandmother disapproved of candy, not because of tooth decay or indigestion, but because children liked it and children should perforce not have anything they liked.

I sniffed happily at the Cherriswete a few times and then gave each girl in my retinue a crumb, not because I liked her but because of her loyalty. Then I took it home, showed it to my little sister, spun it a few times more past her nose to torture her, and divided it with her, since even though young and savage we loved each other very much.

My heart was full. I knew at last that I loved Red. I was his, to steal a phrase. We belonged together, a male and female who understood the gastronomical urge.

I never saw him again, since his father was transferred by Standard Oil from Brea to Shanghai that week end, but he has had much more influence on me with that one Cherriswete than most men could have in twenty years of Pol Roger and lark tongues. Sometimes I wonder if he is still tall, freckled, and irreverent—and if he remembers how to woo a woman. Often I thank him for having, no matter how accidentally, taught me to realize the almost vascular connection between love and lobster pâté, between eating and romance.

I

That kind of milk toast is part of the unwritten cookery book engraved, almost without conscious recognition of it, in the mind of anyone who ever tended the young, the weak, the old. It is a warm, mild, soothing thing, full of innocent strength.

There is no recipe for it in even my homeliest kitchen manuals, in their generally revolting lists under such titles as "Feeding the Sick" and "Invalid Receipts." It is, in other words, an instinctive palliative, something like boiled water. But since some human beings may by dire oversight have missed the ministrations of their grandmothers, or of such a great hulk of woman as cared once for me when I was low in body, I shall print an approximation of the rule, to be adapted naturally to the relative strength or weakness of the person to imbibe it.

Milk Toast
(for the Ill, Weak, Old, Very Young, or Weary)

1 pint milk, part cream if the person is not forbidden that	sweet butter, if butter is allowed
4 slices good bread, preferably homemade	salt, pepper, if not a child or very ill

Heat the milk gently to the simmering point. Meanwhile have ready 4 freshly-toasted slices of bread. Butter them generously. Heat a pretty bowl, deeper than it is wide. Break the hot buttered toast into it, pour the steaming but not boiling milk over it, sprinkle a very little salt and pepper on the top, and serve at once.

It can be seen that compromise lies in every ingredient. The basis for the whole is toasted bread soaked in warm milk. The sweet butter, the seasoning, the cream and the milk—these are sops indeed to the sybarite in even the sickest of us.

I have used this bland prescription more than once upon myself, recognizing a flicker across my cheekbones, a humming near my elbows and my knees, that meant fatigue had crept too close to the fortress walls. I have found partaking of a warm full

bowl of it, in an early bed after a long bath, a very wise medicine—and me but weary, not ill, weak, old, not very young!

And I remember going one night to a famous restaurant, the
quiet, subtly lighted kind like the Chambord, for instance, with
a man who was healthier than almost anyone I ever met, because he had just emerged from months of dreadful illness, the
quiet, subtly mortal kind. He still moved cautiously and spoke
in a somewhat awed voice, and with a courteous but matter-of-
fact apology he ordered milk toast for himself, hinting meanwhile at untold gastronomical delights for me.

I upset him and our waiter, only temporarily however, by
asking for milk toast too, not because of my deep dislike of a
cluttered table, but because I suddenly wanted the clear, com-
forting feel of the brew upon my tongue.

While I drank a glass of sherry an increasing flurry surrounded us. It took me some minutes to realize that probably
never before in the fifty or so years the restaurant had been there
had anyone ordered milk toast—nothing but milk toast. I began to feel as if screens would be whisked up around us, like two
unfortunate or indiscreet athletes on a football field. There was
a mounting air of tension among the waiters, who increased
gradually in our corner of the room from three to about twelve.
By the time the silver chafing dishes had been wheeled before
us, we had three captains, all plainly nervous, eying the maneu-
vers from nearby vantage points.

The thing began: butter sizzling here, toast smoking delicately there, rich milk trembling at the bubbling point but no
further, a huge silver pepper mill held ready, salt, *rock*-salt, in a
Rumanian grinder, paprika in a tin marked "Buda-Pesth."
Helpless, a little hysterical under our super-genteel exteriors,
my friend and I waited. The flames flamed. The three captains
surged into action. And before we could really follow the intricate and apparently well-rehearsed ballet, two mammoth silver

bowls, just like the nursery ones but bigger and more beautiful, steamed before us, and we sat spooning up the most luxurious, most ridiculously and spectacularly delicious milk toast either of us had eaten in our long, full, and at times invalidish lives.

It was a small modern miracle of gastronomy, certainly not worth having illness for, but worth pondering on, in case milk toast might help.

S *is for* Sad

. . . and for the mysterious appetite that often surges in us when our hearts seem about to break and our lives seem too bleakly empty. Like every other physical phenomenon, there is always good reason for this hunger if we are blunt enough to recognize it.

The prettifiers of human passion choose to think that a man who has just watched his true love die is lifted above such ugly things as food, that he is exalted by his grief, that his mind dwells exclusively on thoughts of eternity and the hereafter. The mixture of wails and wassail at an Irish wake is frowned upon as merely an alcoholic excuse by the sticklers for burial etiquette, and the ancient symbolism of funeral baked meats is accepted, somewhat grudgingly, as a pagan custom which has been Christianized sufficiently by our church fathers to justify a good roast of beef and some ice cream and cake after the trip to the family burying ground with Gramp.

The truth is that most bereaved souls crave nourishment more tangible than prayers:[1] they want a steak. What is more, they need a steak. Preferably they need it rare, grilled, heavily salted, for that way it is most easily digested, and most quickly turned into the glandular whip their tired adrenals cry for.

A prime story of this need is the chapter in Thomas Wolfe's *Look Homeward, Angel*, just after Ben has died, when his two racked brothers begin to laugh and joke like young colts, and then go in the dawn to Ben's favorite all-night beanery and eat an enormous, silly meal. Another good example is in D. H. Lawrence's *Sons and Lovers*, as I remember. There are many more, all of them shocking, and yet strangely reassuring too, like some kinds of music.

Perhaps that is because they are true, far past prettiness. They tell us what we then most need to be reminded of, that underneath the anguish of death and pain and ugliness are the facts of hunger and unquenchable life, shining, peaceful. It is as if our bodies, wiser than we who wear them, call out for encouragement and strength and, in spite of us and of the patterns of proper behavior we have learned, compel us to answer, and to eat.

More often than not, in such compulsory feastings, we eat enormously, and that too is good, for we are stupefying ourselves, anesthetizing our overwrought nerves with a heavy dose of proteins, and our bodies will grow sleepy with digestion and let us rest a little after the long vigil.

I tried to say this once to a man who, being well raised and sensitive, was in a state of shock at his behavior.

It was late at night. He had been driving up and down the coastal highway, cautiously and in a numb way almost happily, ever since a little before noon that day when his love had died. She was one of the most beautiful women in the world, and one of the most famous, and he loved her for these reasons and even more so because she loved him too. But he had to watch her die, for two nights and a day.

When she was finally at peace he walked from her bedside like a deaf, blind man, got into his car and headed for the coast, and in the next hours he must have stopped at four or five big restaurants and eaten a thick steak at each one, with other things he usually ignored, like piles of French fried potatoes, slabs of pie, and whatever bread was in front of him. He had a flask of cognac in the car but did not touch it; instead he drank cup after cup of searing black coffee, with or without food, in a dozen little joints along the road, and then left them humming and whistling.

By the time I saw him he was literally bulging and had loosened his belt futilely to make room for the load in his middle. He put his head in his hands and shuddered. "How could I?" he said. "How could I—and she not yet in her coffin!"

It was a helpless protest, and I, more plainspoken than usual, tried to cut through his digestive fog, to tell him how right he had been to let his body lead him on this orgy, how it would tide him over the next hours, how his hunger had made him do what his upbringing had taught him was gross, indelicate, unfeeling.

He soon went to his bed, staggering, hardly conscious, certainly uncaring for a time at least of his own or the world's new woe. But years later, so strong was his training, he would think back on that day with a deep embarrassment, no matter how candidly he admitted the basic wisdom of his behavior. He would always feel, in spite of himself, that sadness should not be connected so directly with gastronomy.

I

Going to a funeral is perhaps even more wearing than watching someone die, and I know of at least one candid admission of this ugly fact. An old French marshal, returning from the elaborate rites for his last contemporary, let servants and his family strip the heavy decorations from him and then said with great dignity, "You may serve me with two roasted pigeons. I have noticed that after eating a brace of them I arise from the table feeling much more resigned."

I imagine, since this happened many years ago, that the birds were braised in good butter, covered closely, and allowed to fret in their own juices until done. (Some, scorning the meat as so much crow, say a pigeon is *never* done. But crow, to yet others, is good.)

Old pigeons, except stewed in a pie, are barely mentioned in kitchen manuals, and even squabs, their tender little chicks, are in none too good gastronomical odor. I agree heartily with the great Escoffier that this is a crying shame, "since when the birds are of excellent quality, they are worthy of the best tables."

I grew interested in them, roasted of course, when I was fairly young. My mother was in the throes of several years of childbearing, which I watched interestedly from the sidelines. My father seemed, except at certain moments quite beyond my youthful understanding, to be quite as ineffectual as I was, and when it was found that grilled squabs might satisfy the troubled, peckish woman, he and I bent with mutual ardor, and an enthusiasm on my part which I do not think he yet recognizes, to satisfy her need.

He bought pigeons. He read books. We discussed the less romantic aspects of mating and breeding. I helped, even more realistically, to maintain the impeccable cotes. We had very fine birds. We even had a few babies, thanks to my father's jealous watchings, waitings, and pigeon-wise suspicions.

But by the time the eggs hatched Mother had lost her yearning for roast squabs: quite plainly it sickened her to hear them named. As for the increasing roar of early morning cooings from the cotes, it drove her nearly frantic.

My father moved the birds down to a ranch in the country and kept on studying, perhaps with vicarious delight, the intricacies of pigeon fidelity. He was always buying new birds, handsome puff-throated males, shimmering sweet little matrons.

As far as I can remember I never ate a single squab. All that remains with me, at least about the edible part of the lengthy experiment, is looking at the little roasted birds that came downstairs untouched on Mother's tray, feeling ready to pounce on them, and hearing her nurse say, "Nupnup*nup*! Mizz Fussbudget may want it later!" I still don't really know who ate those plump juicy little morsels, but I can guess, so appetizing did they look as Nurse flicked them through the door into the darkened kitchen. There was anticipation in every starched crease of her.

A friend of mine who was on the municipal council in a provincial French town studded with architectural gems has told me that there used to be daily battles, every springtime, over whether the pigeons roosting in the church façades and on the statues' heads should be netted and made into a kind of brothy pie for the poor, or left yet another year in their disfiguring filth. The latter alternative always was carried, mainly because it would take more men than the town could muster to kill the birds and clean up their accumulated droppings, and then there would be more pigeon pie than a town of five times that size could eat, poor and rich together, if by some miracle all the birds flew properly into the traps held out for them. The town, thanks to time's unceasing labors, remains just about as limy and beautiful as ever, and its poor are hardly hungrier than they would have been if they had sat down once annually before a Gargantuan pie of an origin so obviously more practical than charitable.

To be truthful, I do not know what I would do if I were presented with, say, twenty-four tough stringy pigeons to make edible. I suppose I would put them in a pie, like the blackbirds, but anything that involves plucking, cleaning, boning, simmering, seasoning, this and that, somewhat discourages me. Perhaps it would be best to make a soup of them, a good heartening broth, with a little sherry in it.

No. Gastronomically undaunted, I would do this, given not

twenty-four but four healthy birds: clean them properly, rub them well with a cut lemon and then a little cloth wet with decent brandy, brown them evenly and well in a mixture of sweet butter and olive oil, and simmer them closely covered for about a half-hour, or until tender.

If I felt fussy and ready for more fussiness, as often happens after a funeral, I would remove the birds to a shallow casserole, put a little brandy over them, and set them alight, to rid them of some of their fat gaminess; and I would reduce the braize and a cup of good red wine to a fine sauce to pour over them, and I would serve them on toasted buttery slices of decent bread.

It sounds good. It does not need a burial to make it so. All it needs, oh, dreadful practicality, is some pigeons!

T *is for*
Turbot

. . . as well as trout, and for me at least these two gastronomical delights will be forever one.

Do I mean turbot, what dictionaries call "a large, flat fish esteemed as food," or do I mean trout, leering up, twisted and blue, from its pan? My confusion, spiritual at least, springs from an experiment with pressure-cookers, which started some time around 1820 near the little French village of Villecrêne, and ended in 1948 near the little American village of Beverly Hills.

One of the pleasantest stories, I think, in one of the pleasantest books ever written, Brillat-Savarin's *Physiology of Taste*, is the anecdote called, very simply, "The Turbot." In it he tells, with a ruminative smugness which he was indeed entitled to, how he saved the day as well as the menaced domestic bliss of two of his dearest friends.

They had invited a group of "pleasant people" to lunch at their country place at Villecrêne on a Sunday, and when Brillat-Savarin arrived on horseback from Paris on Saturday night, as their privileged guest, he found them at polite swords' points over what to do with a magnificent turbot which was, unfortunately, too enormous to fit into any cooking pan.

It would be another hundred years or so before the great Escoffier was to state sternly, "It is of the greatest importance . . . that the turbot not be cooked too long beforehand, since it tends to harden, crumple, and lose its flavor," and the young French couple, happily unconscious of blundering, plainly planned to boil their catch whole and then serve it the next day in its own jelly, with some such sauce as a mayonnaise, probably garnished with little tomatoes and cucumbers from their garden.

Madame stood up stoutly against the chopper which her exasperated husband was threatening to use. The tactful Professor insisted, in spite of feeling ravenously hungry, that the whole household help him immediately in coping with this domestic crisis. He sniffed through the establishment like an eager hound, until in the laundry, of all places, he found exactly what he needed: the copper wash boiler, which of course was solidly a part of its own little furnace. He marshaled the servants into a solemn procession, himself at the head bearing the turbot, the doubting cook and his skeptical friend in the rear, and proceeded to carry out his first dramatic assertion that the fish must, and indeed would, remain in one piece until its final appearance.

While the maids built up a fine fire, and the cook assembled onions, shallots, and highly flavored herbs, he devised a kind of hammock from a large reed clothes hamper. He laid the fresh herbs in a thick layer on the bottom, then the cleaned and salted fish, and then a second layer of herbs.

"Then the hammock was put across the boiler," he wrote, "which was half full of water, and the whole was covered with a small washtub around which we banked dry sand, to keep the steam from escaping too easily. Soon the water was boiling madly; steam filled the inside of the tub, which was removed at the end of a half-hour, and the hammock was taken out of the boiler with the turbot cooked to perfection, white as snow, and most agreeable to look at."

The next day all the guests exclaimed at its handsome appearance, and ". . . it was unanimously agreed that the fish prepared according to my system was incomparably better than if it had been cooked in the traditional turbot-pan . . . [for] since it had not been passed through boiling water it had lost none of its basic qualities, and had on the contrary absorbed all the aroma of the seasoning."

This is so obvious a result of his method that it surprises me to find some such master as Escoffier ignoring its principles and continuing, a century later, to advise his followers to boil turbot in the classical mixture of seven parts salted water to one of sweet milk.

The Professor himself hoped that his system would be followed and developed for the inexpensive and wholesome feeding of large numbers of people, as in armies and institutions, and I should think that hotel cookery as understood by Escoffier would fall somewhere into these categories. Perhaps it did not because pressure-cookers, as we casually know and use them today, were still too risky a utensil when the master chef died in 1934. Whatever the reasons, there can be no doubt that the boiled and/or poached fish generally served in even the best restaurants suffer from too much water and too little taste—too much Escoffier and not enough Professor.

The only real mass harnessing of steam to the pleasures of the table that I know about is done by the Chinese, and I can, in my mind, be at this very minute in the alley doorway of a Cantonese restaurant just off Plymouth Square in San Francisco, watching the exciting rhythm of the steam cookery there.

Ducks and cabbages and bean sprouts and a curled carp are all under the one bell-like top, and a fine vapor rises from it, not mingled, not blurred in savor, as the helper raises and lowers it on a long rope according to the hissed, hectic directions of the cook. The hot room has an airiness about it unknown to most public kitchens, in spite of, or perhaps because of, the controlled clouds of steam.

There is a steady chopping sound: everything edible seems to pass from the shelves to the steam stove by way of the chef's incredibly skilled knife, and fish, fowl, celery, and a hundred other things turn, almost too fast to watch, into the strips, sticks, and mouth-sized morsels proper for eating with chopsticks. It is perhaps the freshness of these foods that sends up such a salutary vapor, like the bottled chlorophyll we buy to sweeten our stale household air. Certainly the high speed at which the food is cooked keeps it still sending off its gases when it is done—and I prove that a dozen times a week when, mouse-like compared to the elephant of a Chinese steam-stove, and like an *écrivisse* to the Professor's fish, my four-quart Presto turns out vegetables for my ever-hungry children.

It interests me to watch their instinctive love of the good smell of the pot just after it has been opened: they cluster like bees around a jam jar, and sniff and smile, and pop into their mouths the beans or zucchini or whatever I have fixed when it is almost too hot to touch. The next day, inevitably, there is much less interest in what is left, since its first fresh flavor has been tainted by time's passage, and I myself, more jaded in palate, find that salt and soy and butter are necessary, where for the first minutes nothing could possibly have been wanted to accentuate the indescribable freshness of the food.

There are a dozen books and a hundred booklets on modern pressure-cookery. I think most of them dull, after the first simple principles have been laid down and shown to be foolproof, to the timid and the superstitious, with a series of artful photographs and charts. Perhaps it is because I can attain such comfortable forgetfulness of my life's problems in the construction of a stew (as some women do in baking bread) that I do not wish to cut the time for it from four hours to forty minutes. And I am not particularly interested in "tenderizing" inferior cuts of meat, being intransigently of the school that would choose one good dinner of prime beef rather than six of thinly disguised chuck.

But for succulent, almost melodramatically delicious vegetables nothing can equal a modern Presto; and since my children live mainly upon the earth's plants, to strengthen them for keener if less nourishing delights, I sharpen their palates thankfully with what comes in a seemingly endless flood from my steam-cooker.

At times, I confess gastronomically, I grow damned bored. And that is when I call up the Professor's ghost, and with a bow to him I make, much more timetakingly than any modern recipe would tolerate, my own modest version of his turbot.

I could not duplicate his, of course, even if I did have the turbot—and an ancient copper boiler in a laundry house. Given the fish (and my Bendix!), where would I find the herbs? But there is the Presto. And there are, thanks to fast trains and efficient fish farms, beautiful almost instant-fresh rainbow trout. And there is my postmaternal necessity for something besides beans and zucchini. There is, finally, my sentimental feeling about Brillat-Savarin himself.

The recipe which I have devoutly evolved,[1] assumes that I have two fresh trout, handsome and alike—a somewhat impertinent assumption on the side of a sage-covered desert hill, but not so much so near the fine markets of Beverly Hills where I first assumed it. Two trout, unfortunately, are all that my cooker will hold. But the best thing about the recipe is that it can be repeated endlessly, and a dozen or so pretty fish, side by side in their clear jelly upon their couch of herbs, is a sight worth any coping, especially when it can be saluted, while the Professor's ghost smiles just over my left shoulder, with a bottle of Wente's Pinot Chardonnay or, dryer and just as cold, Grey Riesling.

Then I can feel, almost as justifiably smug as the old Frenchman when he wrote about his turbot, that I have bolstered my own self-esteem as a cook, if not saved such domestic bliss as he fought for. I can forget the sometimes tiresome routine of nourishing my family, and sit back happily, in the company of One, and eat as artful a combination of fresh natural flavors as ever lay upon a plate. I can compliment myself unashamedly that I have dared ponder on what a gaffer wrote down more than a hundred years ago and have adapted it to such an anachronism-in-reverse as a little aluminum pot with a gauge sticking up, a far cry from the boiler at Villecrêne.

"While my ears drank their fill of the compliments which were showered upon me," Brillat-Savarin wrote contentedly, "my eyes sought out other even more sincere ones in the visible post-mortem verdict of the guests, and I observed with secret satisfaction that General Labassée was so pleased that he smiled anew at each bite, while the curé had his chin stretched upwards and his ecstatic eyes fixed upon the ceiling, and . . . Monsieur Villemain leaned his head with his jaw tipped to the west, like a man who is listening. . . .

"All of this is useful to remember," he went on. And I know how right he was, for though no general has tasted my little offshoot of the famous turbot, and no curé, another good man has—and with me—and I shall remember the usefulness of the recipe many times again, and the magic of its flavors, when I may, being human, have become boresome.

I

Trout Brillat-Savarin

(who said [Aphorism IX], "The invention of a new dish adds more to the happiness of mankind than the discovery of a star.")

⅓ cup water	2 packages plain gelatin
1 small head lettuce	1 cup fish stock (add water if
4 scallions	necessary, to make full cup)
parsley, other fresh herbs at	½ teaspoon salt
discretion	tabasco sauce
2 fine trout	2 cups dry white wine
wine vinegar	¼ cup wine vinegar, optional

Put water in pressure-cooker. Put in the rack. Shred lettuce, mince scallions (tops and all), chop parsley and choice of fresh herbs—enough to make about 4 cups when lightly tossed together. Put mixed greens on rack and lay properly cleaned trout, bellies together and fins affectionately intertwined, on this soft bed.

Follow the procedure that is correct for the make of pressure-cooker being used, and when gauge is at Cook keep it there for 2½ to 3 minutes, no longer.

Put cooker under cold-water stream at once, remove cover as soon as possible, and take out rack holding trout and greens.

Put all juice, strained, into a measuring cup, adding enough cool water to make one full cup. Carefully slide trout on their bed into a shallow oblong casserole or a fish platter. Sprinkle generously with good wine vinegar.

Dissolve the gelatin in the fish stock. Add salt and 2 or 3 drops of tabasco (and the ¼ cup of wine vinegar if a sharp aspic is desired). Bring the 2 cups of dry white wine to the boiling point, no more, and mix well with the stock-gelatin. Allow to cool to the thickening point. Spoon ⅓ of it gently over the trout and shake a little to let it penetrate the herb bed. Place casserole in refrigerator for five minutes or so, then repeat 2 or 3 times, so that the fish will be well covered with a clear jelly. Chill well. Serve with a freshly made and very simple mayonnaise.

Lemon juice can be used instead of wine vinegar, but it may war with the wine, as well as with the delicate nutlike quality of the fish itself. For luncheon it is amusing (I can never use this word, no matter how straightforwardly I mean it, without wincing at the ever-present memory of an early Thurber cartoon in *The New Yorker*, in which two pompous people were apparently awing two timid ones by yammering of "an amusing little wine of the country," or something like that) to use in the aspic a rosé wine rather than a white: it turns it into what more than one good chef calls "a ladies' dish," and the rosé, from Louis Martini or Beaulieu for instance, can be served with the meal.

You must take care not to overcook the fish by even ten seconds or it will "crumple," as Escoffier says of turbot. But in spite of his dictum, this dish can be made the night before it is to be served, although the trout lose something of their shimmer in such a wait, as perhaps the Professor's turbot at Villecrêne did not.

U *is for*
Universal

. . . and for a fleeting discussion of bread and salt, which remains man's universal meal in spite of the understandable assumption that it may instead be restaurant sauce, as served from Singapore to Buenos Aires and back again in any upper-class chophouse.

There is a special and unmistakable liquid, a staple of the chef who must maintain his so-called standards but still is too busy to start afresh for each patron which at this very moment is being doused indiscriminately upon veal cutlets, fillets of beef, and even slices of salmon in uncountable kitchens all over the world. It is thinner than thick, browner than red, a consummate mixture of mediocrity that baffles and impresses the ignorant and nauseates the knowing. Its sparing use denotes a clever restaurant cook, its prodigality a reckless one, for even the dullest diner will in the end revolt and go elsewhere if every entrée he orders swims in the same questionable flood.

It may serve one good purpose: any homesick wanderer can, with one mouthful of it in Detroit, be back in any almost identical eating house in Plymouth, Bombay, or Lima, snug in his nostalgic memories of other steaks or cutlets that tasted just the same!

Perhaps gastronomers of a few hundred years from now will consider it the Universal Food of our century. Meanwhile I prefer to think of an older and much simpler one: the bread that has been broken, for countless years, and the salt that has been eaten with it, as well as sprinkled over the doorsteps of our ancestors and offered with incense to the gods, even unto now.

Salt, sodium chloride, NaCl, is perhaps too much a part of today's table, or so at least many of our doctors feel,[1] and rightly when they can point to patients with hardened arteries and palsy, and less often but with equal poignancy to the palate-deadened children and traveling salesmen and such who whip themselves at every meal the way a cow must in the spring, licking at salt to stimulate her glands.

It has always been vegetable and cereal eaters, cows and humankind alike, who most crave the taste of salt, and men who live on roasted meat, like the Bedouins, need never touch it, for natural flavors can appease them without any help. But once meat is boiled, with its goodness in part drained from it, salt must be added to make it decently palatable. There is a sensual satisfaction about the rough bitter crystals of rock salt that are sprinkled over a true pot-au-feu or bouilli, at least as I used to eat it in Burgundy, that no grilled kid could equal, and yet I have never put salt on beef to be seared and roasted over the coals in my patio barbecue, and people who in restaurants would automatically reach for the saltcellar eat it blissfully, incredulous when at the end they learn what they have done.

I was taught when very young that it is an insult to the cook to salt a dish before it has been tasted, and in spite of my adult knowledge of the reasons for such an unthinking gesture I still resent it when anyone at my table seasons something as soon as it is put before him. I know that his tongue is jaded, calloused even, by restaurant sauces and a thousand dinners that have had to be heightened with anything at hand in order to be swallowed at all. Still I wish, silently most of the time, that he would take a chance and eat just one bite before he sprinkles the ubiquitous salt and pepper upon whatever has been prepared for him. I have great pride in my culinary knowingness, and feel, with good proof, that some things need salt and some do not. Green beans, for instance, as opposed to my patio steak: the first needs an ample touch of salt, ample sweet butter, and then an ample grind of fresh pepper, while the second never sees anything but herbs and wine.

Bread is another thing again, a cereal which in one way or another carries itself most easily with salt somewhere about it. I know a man of parts who, when he eats reddish-brown Russian rye bread, will spread it thickly with sweet butter and then, to my own private horror, coat the whole with an impossible load of table salt; he likes the odor, texture, taste; it makes him feel good to eat this honest, enriching fare.

Bread made without salt has a strange sweetness about it, almost a nutmeg taste, much more of a chemical difference than the one small omission would be expected to make. And in the making it does not smell as yeasty and irresistible somehow. It is worth the bother, if indeed it can be called bother to mix the whole and then pound it and let it rise and pound it, in the age-old ritual of "baking."

It is too bad, I think, that fewer and fewer people try its classical rhythm. It brings a mysterious satisfaction with it, which I saw not long ago when a fine woman was told never to touch salt again, and suddenly her whole house became more peaceful, all because the cook had to make salt-free bread twice weekly.

The cook herself was drunk less often, for having to concentrate and remember: breadmaking is not a quarter-hour task like pie crust or dumplings.

The fine woman's fine husband came home oftener, and

sniffed happily at the round pan of dough, a clean linen napkin laid lightly over it, rising on a dining room chair near the furnace register.

People too, not just husbands, came in on baking days and sat, and no matter what their financial brackets, they leaned back gladly to eat a slice or two or three of the warm delicious fresh-baked loaf, and taste its strange sweetness, and never miss the salt that supposedly should make it palatable.

The fine woman told me that the accident of being forbidden ever to taste salt again had made her very happy, because of the bread-baking, and I know what she meant. Few people now are forced, as she was, to make their own loaves, and even fewer to forego the seasoning which has become a modern gastronomical necessity but should still be, according to the laws of nature, a privilege dictated by position, the priests, and the time of year.

A cook who must rely upon his own skill to make something edible, rather than toss in an impossible load of salt in the hope that it will stupefy if not soothe the outraged palates of his guests, can count himself fortunate indeed, for there is no culinary challenge quite as demanding as salt-free food in the modern diet. It can be good food, as I know. It can in the end wreak a strange revenge and make most other dishes in most other dining places taste ghoulishly pickled and cadaverous, like warmed-over slices of zombie.

There are a thousand tricks at hand, of course, to make saltless food full enough of natural flavor to be satisfying. The most helpful one in present-day kitchens is the pressure-cooker, which if intelligently used can turn out such things as garden peas with a God-given flavor unfamiliar to most modern tongues.

In general the simplest procedures are the best, and a cook who finds himself by force or his own choice in a salt-free kitchen will soon revert to an almost primitive way of roasting, basting, and poaching. He will also, if he is worth his forbidden salt, think back on his own more ornate skills and dream of a perfect Soubise the way some men dream of virgins. And he will, and this I can swear to, next make that Soubise with a tenderness and respect unknown to him in the old days when he did it daily, and at times overcasually, assuming with most of his clients that too much of a good thing might be a sin but was still more desirable than not enough of it.

I am convinced that coping with a saltless regimen should be part of every good chef's schedule, at least once a year or so, to sharpen his dulled appreciation of food's basic flavors and make him consider them with caution before his routine boiling and peeling. In a strange kitchen-fashion some such penance as this might act as a kind of purification, connected in its own way with the religious significance that has always cloaked bread and salt.

Having made honest bread again,[2] with or without salt, and recollected its mysterious moving fragrance; having grilled meat again,[3] untainted by the chemistry of salt, the cook would be able to sense fundamental flavors that are quite beyond too many of us, and would be refreshed, strengthened, able once more to make his cunning sauces without stooping, as he has found it increasingly easy to do, to the universal brew, the one served in so many restaurants, the one recognizable from here to there.

He would, knowing it or not, remember that salt and bread are to be honored, not turned into dull necessity and the puffed packaged furnishings of any corner grocery. He would be a better cook.

I

When I was younger, and less set in my sensory patterns than I am now, I was impatient of people who rebelled, more or less helplessly, at a doctor's dictum that they must forego cigarettes, or desserts, or, most especially, salt.

Although it is something I myself could be told never to taste again and still manage to live pleasurably, I am more tolerant to-day of diabetics who risk sure death for a secret orgy of banana cream pie, or heart cases who fret and even weep a little at the ghastly flatness, or so it seems to them, of a salt-sodium-free diet. My sympathy, as I approach the stiffer years, grows more compassionate.

One reason most people protest so passionately against giving up salt is that they, like morphine addicts, have set up almost miraculous tolerance, thanks to its indiscriminate use in modern cookery, to the lack of natural flavor or to camouflaged carelessness.

It is impossible to conceive of average-to-good restaurant food, say, some completely simple thing like scrambled eggs with spinach, which would be much more than edible without a double dose of salt, the one slapped in automatically by the chef, the other sprinkled in almost as automatically by the diner. As for home-cooking, too often food is drained of its inherent goodness by overcooking, by throwing away its natural juices, by a hundred things which could be remedied with a little thought.

And thus it is that when, as in the case of a fine friend of mine, the outraged human body cries no, no to such cumulative excess as we take for granted, there is a rebellion of the palate, as drastic in its way as the violent battle of nausea and agony that a dipsomaniac puts up, or a cocaine-sniffer, and in spite of himself too, when he is deprived of his poison.

The substitutes for salt are many, and pathetically interesting. They come in powder or liquid form, to be sprinkled at will upon the food which is at first so tasteless, and which will remain that way if unintelligently prepared. They have a dozen different names, most impressive, and although the powder form, for instance, can easily be put into a regular salt shaker and used without comment, I have noticed that most heart patients prefer to keep it in its dramatically blunt little bottle, with the elaborate formula marked plainly if cryptically upon it, and to say with self-pitying resignation to their nurses or husbands or dutiful daughters, "Please pass me my Ceo-Nurtasode" instead of ". . . the salt."

The plainly printed ingredients of such a gastronomical stopgap are equally soul-satisfying psychologically. Instead of sodium chloride, which is about all that would be mentioned on a pharmacist's label for plain table salt, there is a handsome list of mysterious and at times unpronounceable chemicals: ammonium and potassium chlorides, calcium and potassium formates, magnesium citrates, on and on, increasingly polysyllabic.

It is fun, in a sad way, to cloak monotony in such giddiness. This bottled powder, though, makes vegetables taste bitter; that colorless liquid, a teaspoonful to a loaf, makes bread taste no better than if it were blankly saltless. Hohum, the salt-free sufferer finally murmurs, hohum, enough of *that*!

There is, it seems, no substitute for NaCl. There is no faking its fine stimulus, its artful aid—except to use it with more respectful attention to its basic powers and dangers; except, perhaps, to taste it for a change, instead of taking it for granted.

2

There are as many good recipes for bread as there are good cookbooks, a statement not quite as equivocal as it at first sounds, for there are indeed formidable numbers of honest collections of the basic rules of cookery: Fanny Farmer's, Mrs.

Simon Kander's, Mrs. Rombauer's, Louis de Gouy's, Louis Diat's, and on and on, just here in America.

Of course national and racial differences are at times in conflict, and an Italian recipe for bread, or a French one, will astound and amuse a housewife in Kansas who has learned the weekly rhythm of the baking from her Great-Aunt Maggie. I have watched polite Mexicans almost gag on the "American bread" my brother brought down to Chapala from Guadalajara's one fancy grocery as a special treat for them, as an exotic as well as optimistically healthful change from their tortillas, so flat and sandy-dry.

Breadmaking, I have found, is a very personal thing, and what one cook does another cannot or will not do because it does not feel right. Fortunately for the cook's vanity as well as the consumer's appetite, *good* bread can never be anything but that, whether the dough rose twice or thrice, whether the yeast worked in a Yorkshire buttery or on a California cellar shelf. *Good* bread will forever send out its own mysterious and magical goodness, to all the senses, and quite aside from all the cookbooks, perhaps the best way to learn how to make it is to ask an old, wise, and, above all, *good* woman.

3

This recipe is anyone's for the taking. It presupposes a simple outdoor grill, but can be followed in a kitchen (also presupposing inevitable clouds of almost choking but still delicious blue smoke).

The kitchen grill should be *very hot*. The outdoor fire should be reduced to a good bed of lively, glowing coals. The ingredients are simple, as is the practiced routine which pulls them into focus. The result is, inevitably, a happy one, at least for Occasions: it is not the kind to expect too often, having something magnificent and sacrificial about it in a primitive way.

INGREDIENTS (*for 5-pound sirloin steak*)

1 steak, at least 2 and
preferably 3 inches thick.
(Sirloin is best; fillet is too
tender.)
6 cloves garlic
¾ cup good olive oil
¾ cup soy sauce

½ pound unsalted butter
2 cups finely chopped scallions,
green pepper, celery,
parsley, fresh basil if
available
3 cups good plain red table
wine

METHOD

Remove meat from refrigerator at least 4 hours before you need it. Cut off almost all fat, otherwise it will catch on fire. Slash edges ¼ inch deep, every 2 inches, to avoid curling. Skewer tail of steak firmly around bone to insure even broiling, and if it is still loose-looking, bind it around with stout twine. (This will burn off, but by the time it does the meat will have taken its final shape.)

Rub sturdily with peeled and halved garlic cloves on all surfaces, including the bone and what little fat is left.

Put meat into shallow casserole, lying flat, and rub half of soy sauce thoroughly into the upper side. Let stand uncovered. In about an hour turn over and rub the other side. This makes a tough-looking dark coat. Then pour the olive oil on the steak and turn it over two or three times before dinner. (The soy sauce may seem a concession to salt-lovers but is not: it acts as a kind of innocent tanning, and is wonderful on fish, used in the same way.)

Put the chopped vegetables and herbs, the butter and the wine, into a bowl over a very low flame about an hour before dinner, or at the back of the outdoor grill. (¼ cup oyster sauce or Worcestershire sauce can be added at end—not necessary, but good.)

About 20 minutes (rare) to 35 minutes (well-done) before dinner is to be served (this takes a bit of practice in outdoor cookery, to time the right combination of intense heat minus any flame), put the steak on the grill, near which you are standing ready in asbestos or very thick gardening gloves, armed with a whisk broom and a bowl of water to douse the flames (very exciting).

Pour the heated sauce into the casserole containing the remaining oil and soy sauce and put near the coals to bubble.

Turn the steak once or twice by hand, so as not to pierce the shell of seared meat.

When done, lift into the hot casserole of sauce. Slice in fairly thick (about ½ inch) slices into the sauce and douse each one well in it before serving. Slices that are too rare will cook if left in the sauce a minute or so.

This somewhat primeval dish is easy to prepare, once practiced. I always serve it generously, with equally generous baskets of lightly toasted sourdough bread (for sopping), piles of fresh watercress in wooden bowls, platters of thickly sliced tomatoes (innocent of anything but a possible sprinkling of chopped fresh basil), and ample Tipo Red or ale. I used to have cheeses later, for what was left of the bread, but I have found that a basket of cool fresh fruit and cups of strong "Louisiana" coffee are more welcome to the pleasantly stimulated and at the same time surfeited diners.

V is for
Venality

. . . and for the mixture of gastronomical pleasure and corruption that helps senators and actresses pounce with such slyly hidden skill upon their prey.

Wherever politics are played, of no matter what color, sex, or reason, the table is an intrinsic part of them, so much so that Brillat-Savarin asserted, enthusiastically if not too correctly, that every great event in history has been consummated over a banquet board. Though I may question his statement, I still admit the loose rightness of it and bow to the companion thought that history is indeed largely venal, no matter what its ultimate nobility. Surely many a soldier has been saved from death because his general slept the night before the battle with Ottilia instead of Claudia, and more than one pretty creature in a Hollywood restaurant has missed stardom but kept her female balance because a producer did not like the way she ate asparagus.

Wherever politics are played, then, which means wherever in the world more than five men foregather, venality sits at table with them, corrupt, all-powerful. In every city from Oskaloosa to Madrid, there is one meeting place which above all others furthers and comforts the inevitable progress of the evil-bent, and the ghost of a Paris senator who last lunched at Foyot's in 1897 would find itself perfectly at home in a certain air-conditioned restaurant in Washington, this year or next, or in some such place as Mike Romanoff's[1] in Beverly Hills.

Some of the best food in America can be, and occasionally is, found at his eating place, although architecture rather than gas-tronomy seems at first glance to be what makes it a necessary part of the nourishment of Hollywood politicians.

The perfection of a rack of lamb served from Mike's over-poweringly beautiful silver meat cart is unimportant; it is where that lamb is consumed that matters. And the interior of this all-important chophouse is so cunningly arranged that its zigzag windowed partitions change it from a long dull store building into a series of rigidly protected social levels.

There are the few tables by the bar, known as Stockholders' Row, and with much of the well-padded comfortable aura of an exclusive club. Probably fifty people in the whole world are qualified to sit at them, and any slight deviation from the twice-daily pattern of familiar paunches causes as much local specu-lation as a mysterious drop in the market.

Then there is the Reinhardt Room, named for its professorial and omnipotent head-captain. It was rightly ignored at first be-cause of its unbecoming pink sides and its dull isolation, until large peepholes were cut in the wall nearest the bar and a cele-brated columnist was prevailed upon with true Romanoff tact to make it the center of her sharpest operations. Now anyone in Hollywood is glad to lunch or dine there, in order to catch her eye, and nod and smile, and guarantee himself one more kind printed word.

Off Reinhardt's stronghold and down a step or two, but still with low partitions so that no Keneth Hopkins hat, no famous toupee, need be missed by a quick-eyed loiterer at the bar, is a small quiet room where big deals are made. There fading stars form independent companies with other people's fortunes and themselves as writer-director-producers. Story editors buy unwritten masterpieces for a quarter of a million. Agents murder other agents with invisible bloodshed.

In spite of the fact that the silver meat cart is too luxuriously weighty to go down the steps, rack of lamb tastes better in the quiet little room, temporarily at least, than anywhere except Stockholders' Row. Certainly it would taste infinitely better there, basted with cyanide and laced with strychnine and garnished with Paris green, than it ever could if by some trick it were served plain and unpoisoned to the star or the story editor or the agent in the Back Room!

The Back Room, quite simply, is suicide. It used to be the whole restaurant, and a few old-timers smile fondly if discreetly at the remembrance of its early days, when Romanoff had not quite enough money to buy chairs and tables for it, and it was cut off from the half-deserted bar by long, gloomy curtains that flapped dismally in the draughts of debt and insecurity and emptiness. That was before Prince Mike and his loyal architect, in mutual desperation, had evolved their fantastically successful scheme of separating the local dukes, cabinet ministers, and lesser nobility into their proper groups, and their fair ladies into the correctly improper ones. Now the room, the dread Back Room, is reserved for a few miserable people whose options have just been dropped and a blissfully ignorant flow of Eastern visitors who do not realize that they are actually enjoying what to a local inhabitant would mean social death.

Well-groomed matrons from the hinterland chatter brightly over excellent cocktails and down great quantities of delicious pastries served with skill and tact, never suspecting that from the Row, and the Reinhardt room, and even from the far-west quiet corner where big deals are made, any glances that may come their way are heavy with scorn, boredom, or at best a faint pity.

Producers shudder at the thought of ever stepping over the sill of that airy pleasant limbo. Producers' girl friends in very new mink coats shudder at the chance that some crowded day they might have to sit two tables in. Ambitious and "promising young" writers of no matter what age recognize the ugly truth that in a pinch they might penetrate as far as the third small table to the left, but pray that it will never be necessary. And meanwhile the happy visitors from Iowa and New York sip and chatter under the same artful roof with countless movie-great, oblivious of their wretched lot—and of one other room, which perhaps even the aristocracy up front might envy: a cool trellised garden off the kitchens, where one day I saw waiters and cooks and the lowliest busboys sitting at a long clean table in the dappled light, eating amicably together without benefit of silver meat cart but from bowls and platters that looked well laden.

Mike Romanoff and his architect had built exceedingly well, I thought with my own kind of snobbism. And I wondered if there, and at the Chambord still, and once at Foyot's, and once at the place in Amsterdam where there were, before the bombs fell, strawberries served two by enormous two upon white damask napkins, and at a hundred other great restaurants around the globe, venality and all its hugger-mugger of intricate play upon the senses did indeed work maggot-like through the kitchens as well as the bar and the Reinhardt Room. I looked at the men and boys eating with such seeming friendliness and pleasure under the vine leaves, and wondered if, for them, cuts of smuggled venison and truffles en papillote took the place of red-haired actresses, of senators of the Opposition, to be manipulated and wooed in the full sense of the word venal. It was harder to believe, there in the sunlight, than it could have been elsewhere.

I

Royal kitchens have always been great ones, gastronomically speaking, although the monarchs themselves have seldom been reputable gourmets. Their power, their more or less ill-gotten means, have made them a mecca for ambitious culinary artists, and there is, in most classical cookbooks, a fairly high level of dishes named after the various kings to whom masterpieces must from time to time be dedicated. Fortunately many such regal dishes are quite simple concoctions, perhaps because the rulers smiled on them in blessed relief after too many headier ones presented to them as a matter of course.

There is, for instance, the delightful dessert named Raspberries Romanoff, which as far as I know has never been served in Prince Mike's Beverly Hills chophouse, nor even in the Winter Palace in St. Petersburg. And there is riz à l'Impératrice: probably I should know for what empress it was presumably first made, but I suspect, being culinarily cynical, that some fair version of it has existed through many a European reign, fresh-named for each, since rice first appeared in the regal cupboards.

There are many good recipes now in circulation for this dish, varying slightly according to the whims of their editors. Fundamentally they follow so closely the nostalgic description given to me by a man to whom riz à l'Impératrice was inextricably a part of great family festivals, with his grandparents' old-school German cooks at the helm, that I can do no better than repeat what he has said.

It was very pretty indeed he said, a not-too-sweet, indescribably light ring of molded rice, vanilla flavored and very suave with custard and whipped heavy cream, with a hint of kirschwasser and tiny bits of minced candied fruits. When the stiff but delicate mold was tipped out upon its platter, there was, magically to a hungry child, red currant jelly on the top, which flowed down over the rich creamy pudding. Ah, it was pretty, the man sighed, not feeling at all silly in his rush of infantile delight.

There may have been a taste of apricot in the rice, he added slowly, evoking from so far back the perfection upon his tongue. (He was right: there should be equal parts of apricot jam and chopped candied fruits stirred into the vanilla-flavored rice before adding the thick custard and the beaten cream.)

But it was the delicate tartness of the currant jelly, opposed to the bland sweetness of the rice, that haunted him most powerfully and made him in the end look so far backward upon his own gastronomical self that I left him, an intruder. . . .

As for the raspberries loftily called Romanoff, they are one variation, and to my mind the best, of a hundred more or less complicated ways of combining fresh fruits and fresh cream. Many other fruits will do, but raspberries seem perfect, when they are indeed fresh and dead-ripe and preferably not touched by water, as they can be when grown in a country garden, whether in Russia, Connecticut, or Savoy (where I first tasted them this way).

Raspberries Romanoff

1 pint carefully sorted raspberries	¼ cup powdered sugar
	¼ cup kirsch
1½ cups heavy cream	

Chill berries. Beat cream stiff, gradually adding sugar and kirsch. Mix lightly with berries, chill thoroughly, and serve in tall thin glasses, with thin unsugared wafers if desired.

W *is for*
Wanton

. . . and the great difference between the way a man eats, and has his doxy eat, when he plans to lead her to the nearest couch, and the way a woman will feed a man for the same end.

A man is much more straightforward—usually. He believes with the unreasoning intuition of a cat or a wolf that he must be strong for the fray and that strength comes from meat: he orders rare steak, with plenty of potatoes alongside, and perhaps a pastry afterward. He may have heard that oysters or a glass of port work aphrodisiacal wonders, more on himself than on The Little Woman, or in an unusual attempt at subtlety augmented by something he vaguely remembers from an old movie he may provide a glass or two of champagne, but in general his gastronomical as well as alcoholic approach to the delights of love is an uncomplicated one which has almost nothing to do with the pleasurable preparation of his companion.

A woman contemplating seduction, on the other hand, is wanton, and a wanton woman, according to the dictionary, is unchaste, licentious, and lewd. This definition obviously applies to her moral rather than her culinary side. Considered solely in connection with the pleasures of the table, a wanton woman is one who with cunning and deliberation prepares a meal which will draw another person to her. The reasons she does so may be anything from political to polite, but her basic acknowledgment that sexual play can be a sure aftermath of gastronomical bliss dictates the game, from the first invitation to the final mouthful of ginger omelet.

It is an agelong rumor, apparently fairly well founded, that the great procuresses and madams have always been the great teachers in "*la cuisine d'amour*." Such proficient pupils as Du Barry and the Countess of Louveciennes bear out this theory, and recipes ascribed to both of them are reprinted annually in various undercover publications dedicated to the somewhat dubious encouragement of libertinage.[1]

Most of the culinary secrets told in them, at a high price and "in plain wrappers for mailing," lean heavily on the timeworn knowledge that dishes made with a great deal of mustard and paprika and other heating spices, and ones based on the generous use of shrimps and other fish high in phosphorus, are usually exciting to both human sexes but particularly to the male. Sometimes a more complicated significance, straight from Freud, is given to recipes thought of long before his day. The dish of eel innocently prepared for a gathering of good pastors by a former brothel cook, which Brillat-Savarin describes so lightly in his *Physiology of Taste*, is a perfect example of this: there is a phallic rightness about the whole thing, visual as well as spiritual, which has more to do with the structure of the fish than the possible presence of a mysterious and exotic spice.

In general, however, the great courtesans have paid less attention to the Freudian appearance of their kitchens' masterpieces, from what I can gather, than to the temperaments of the men they have willed to please. They have studied the appetites of their prey.

This is, in a way, a paraphrase of the old saying, "First catch your hare, then cook him": wolf or even goose can be substituted for the little wild rabbit.

Once caught, a human male is studied by the huntress as thoroughly as if he were a diamond. She looks at his ear lobes and his fingernails after he has eaten of rare beef, and if the former are plump and ruddy, and the latter rosy pink, she knows his glands to be both satisfied and active. She analyzes his motor reflexes after he has downed a fair portion of jugged venison, and if instead of showing a pleasurable skittishness he yawns and puffs and blinks, she nevermore serves that gamy dish. She notes coldly, calculatingly, his reactions to wine and ale and heady spirits, as well as to fruits, eggs, cucumbers, and such; she learns his dietetic tolerance, in short, and his rate of metabolism, and his tendencies toward gastric as well as emotional indigestion. And all this happens whether she be a designing farm girl in Arkansas or a slim worldly beauty on the Cap d'Antibes.

Now I myself am neither of these. I have met a few famous madams, but for one reason or another have never discussed the gastronomy of love with them. I have read a great many books. I have watched a great many people, and fed them too. And here is how I would go about it, as of today, if I wanted to ensnare an average man and lead him, with proper discretion, to the marriage bed. (I say average. The truth is that I do not know a really average man, gastronomically or otherwise. A further complication is that I would quite probably be uninterested in one if ever I met him.)

Given the fact that I have found a male of about my own age, healthy, not too nervous, fairly literate, in other words, one I would like to have cleave unto me for reasons of pleasure if not reproduction: I would soon discover his likes ("First catch your wolf . . ."), and more gradually his dislikes, the deep-seated kind based on the fact that his grandmother made him eat cold turkey one day when it thundered, and his father once called stuffed goose's neck rattlesnake meat, and that sort of thing.

By then I would know what he thought he admired and what he *really* did. If he fancied himself as a bored diner-out I would gradually tease and excite him by bewilderment, and serve him what he thought he hated, in a quiet, lonely room. If he thought he could not possibly eat anything with onion in it I would prove my own control of the situation without his knowing it and prepare a few artful dishes to lead him to realize that he now loved what he had most abhorred. If he hated company I would insinuate two or three or even five arresting characters into his prandial pattern.

In other words I would quarrel with him, on a celestially gentle plane.

I would placate his early inhibitions, and flatter his later ones, and in the end I would have educated him without pain to the point where some such menu as the following would culminate in the flowering of mutual desire, whether social, financial, or impurely intramural:

Good Scotch and water for him, and a very dry Martini for me.

A hot soup made of equal parts of clam juice, chicken broth, and dry white wine, heated just to the simmer.

A light curry of shrimps or crayfish tails. The fish must be peeled raw, soaked in rich milk, and drained, and the sauce must be made of this milk, and the fish poached for at best six minutes in the delicately flavored liquid. This is a reliable trick.

Rice for the curry, and a bland green salad—that is, with a

plain French dressing containing more than its fair share of oil.

A dessert based on chilled cooked fruits, with a seemingly innocent sauce made of honey, whole cinnamon, and brandy, poured over and around them at boiling point and allowed to chill.

By preference I would serve a moderately dry champagne, from the curry on through the last course. If I had no champagne I would produce a bottle of some light chilled wine like a Krug Traminer, since it would be stimulating without going dead once swallowed, as most of the beers and ales do which might superficially seem more desirable. I would serve coffee in great moderation, to put it bluntly, lest it dampen the fire with cold reason.

Thus, depending on the man, the surroundings, and the general conditions of light and shade, I would go about my business—in a time-honored gastronomical fashion which indeed has much of the wanton and therefore unchaste about it, more in the telling than in the dreamed performance, but which still need not be either lewd or vulgarly licentious, at least in one woman's lexicon.

1

Here it seemed a good time, and place, to consult a few friends whose amorous experience was admittedly wider than my own. Instead of asking their opinions on aphrodisiacal gastronomy, however, I managed to astound them by demanding the reverse side: the dishes, meals, drinks, which had proved most likely to dismay them, couchward.

It was agreed, and in my own timid way I must concur, that there is no true whip to love except the need itself, which needs no whip. That is, if two people wish, hope, plan, to be together, they need have no fear of what they must eat first, and indeed no interest in it. Provided they do not eat and drink too much, which there is little risk of their doing if the other hunger be urgent and strong enough, they are as it were impervious to the throes of postprandial digestion. They can eat lobster, rarebit, oysters, tenderloin, and even cold pudding, and will arise undismayed.

On the other hand, flickering passion that must be fanned by a deliberate conglomeration of spices, perfumes, shaded pink candelabra, muted gypsy music, and stretched satin underpinnings, is in a delicate state, most easily nourished and strengthened by the frank admission that autosuggestion is more important than proteins, temporarily at least. This form of hypnosis, no matter how delicious its results, was not what interested me in my naïve census-taking: I wanted to know what would most quickly and completely down my aides.

One said overeagerness for something too long wanted, which I pointed out to him had no necessarily gastronomical connotation, to which he replied that when he was nine he yearned for a Christmas orange more than ever he had since for a woman, and that when he finally got it and bit into it he was as sick as a little pig.

I had no answer to this Jesuitry, so I turned with genteel determination toward a more forthright lover of fair ladies. He supported the theory that nothing can stop true passion, but that an unfortunately chosen dish can form a distinct hazard in the smooth path toward its consummation. When urged, he sketched in with discreet brevity the picture of a male invited by a female to sup with her; he arrived shaved and laved, dallied hopefully over a predinner drink or two, and then was sat down before the one thing in the world he most actively loathed the thought of eating, in his case okra (another and another of my helpers spoke up: avocados, one said in vicarious anguish, kidneys said another). Love hopefully turned to lust, and then lust itself dwindled.

Early training forbade my further questions, but as I am somewhat impatient of such sad, adamant prejudices, I cannot help wondering if a strong enough passion might not sur-mount even a detested flavor, the okra or avocado, even the kid-neys en brochette or in a crisp little artful pie. It seems to me that if a mature, otherwise sensible man turned resolutely from me because he was served with something his mother or his gov-erness had shuddered away from a generation earlier, I would feel myself none too irresistible and would, quite candidly, look elsewhere.

Such surmises, happily, are neither my meat nor my poison, and I can only hope, with all possible philosophy, that fewer and fewer of my fellow men will need to retreat from battle with some such excuse as the look, taste, or smell of a dished overture to another equally basic form of nourishment. I have watched youths and maidens, physically beautiful no matter how boring otherwise, lap up with catlike wisdom a few loathsome ham-burgers at a drive-in before going bluntly into the hill country under the moon. I have also watched, perhaps with more curi-osity because of the perverse quality of the outcome, producer and star, who would eagerly consent to being billed as satyr and nymph but would more aptly qualify as tired-old-dyspeptic and faded-dope, seat themselves in a good restaurant with all the refined smirks, pattings, and ocular caresses of an expur-gated page from *Nana*, and then nibble this, sip that, with the deliberate sly caution of children who have been promised that if they wash the front steps every Saturday they will get their heart's desire for Christmas.

I doubt that they ever do, and a dingy hint of suspicion in even the most amorous, oysterish eye, the coyest café smile, strengthens that doubt.

No matter what shrewd compound from an old whore's cookery book might be produced for them, or for their likes in any walks of life; no matter what revivifying wine or tonic water could be poured for them; no matter, in the end, what spiced essences they spilled upon themselves in the hope of future flames, it would be futile if there was no hunger or lust stronger than their physical ennui, their worldly exhaustion. Something beyond gastronomical boundaries must then take over: the pharmacopoeia of passion.

This special medal has its other side. A wanton woman who could knowingly lead a man toward bed might just as easily, according to my talkative advisers, turn him away from it; and perhaps a whole dictionary of non-love should be written, about how to prepare this and that food most sure to stem desire—kidneys, okra, and avocado, all of them sur canapés d'hier-soir. I myself, imagining one man I would like to woo, can easily invent a menu that would floor him like a stunned ox, and turn him, no matter how unwittingly on his part, into a slumberous lump of masculine inactivity. It is based on what I already know of his physical reactions, as any such plan must be.

I would serve one too many Martinis, that is, about three. Then while his appetite raged, thus whipped with alcohol, I would have generous, rich, salty Italian hors d'oeuvres: prosciutto, little chilled marinated shrimps, olives stuffed with anchovy, spiced and pickled tomatoes—things that would lead him on. Next would come something he no longer wanted but could not resist, something like a ragout of venison, or squabs stuffed with mushrooms and wild rice, and plenty of red wine, sure danger after the cocktails and the highly salted appetizers. I would waste no time on a salad, unless perhaps a freakish rich one treacherously containing truffles and new potatoes. The dessert would be cold, superficially refreshing and tempting, but venomous: a chilled bowl of figs soaked in kirsch, with heavy cream. There would be a small bottle of a Sauterne, sly and icy, or a judicious bit of champagne, and then a small cup of coffee so black and bitter that my victim could not down it, even therapeutically.

All of this would be beautiful fare in itself and in another part of time and space. Here and now it would be sure poison—given the right man. I would, to put it mildly, rest inviolate.

What a hideous plan!

It could be called:

HOW TO UN-SEDUCE

(recipe above)

X *is for*
Xanthippe

. . . and the sure way any shrewish woman can put poison in the pot for her mate, whether or no he be as wise as Socrates and call her Xanthippean or merely Sarah-Jane-ish or Francescan, routinely vituperative or merely undergoing "one of her bad days."

Probably no strychnine has sent as many husbands into their graves as mealtime scolding has, and nothing has driven more men into the arms of other women than the sound of a shrill whine at table. Xanthippe's skill at being ill tempered is largely legendary, and I do not know how much of her nastiness took place over the daily food she served forth to Socrates, but I am convinced that there is no better culture for the quick growth of the germs of marital loathings than the family board. Even the bed must cede position to it, for nighttime and the occasional surcease of physical fatigue and languor can temper mean words there. Nothing alleviates the shock of nagging over an omelet and a salad.[1]

Brillat-Savarin has said as much, and most straightforwardly. But each of us has the right to add his own version of it, and as a two-time widow, both grass and sod, I can vouch for the fact that every man who ever confided in me, as all men eventually will to a seemingly lone woman, that he has not been well understood by his wife, has in the end confessed that try as he would to come home patient and kind for dinner, Sarah-Jane or Frances would serve it forth to him with such a mishmash of scowls and scoldings that he must, to save himself, flee from her.

There are, of course, many sides to this problem, as to all, and I can and do understand Xanthippe's. The main thing to do, in my way of thinking, is to strike an amicable if not truly easy relationship, with full admission that the husband may be basically weary of his wife and the wife fed to the teeth with him. I know several such arrangements, questionably right from a moral point of view (or sentimental!) and made for a hundred reasons from the most venal to the vaguest, and if they be done intelligently they can and do succeed.

The reason I advocate this tacit admission of extramural satisfactions and intramural tolerance is that people must eat. It is true that they must also make love, and in order to do so must in one way or another make money. But the most important of these functions, to my mind, is the eating. Neither of the others can be done well without it: an impoverished man is hungry, and a hungry man, as too many dictators have proved, is not a reproductive and perforce sexually keen fellow. That is why I think that food is the most important of our three basic needs, and why I do deplore its poisoning, its deadly contamination, by anything as vicious as bad temper.

Socrates escaped from Xanthippe in ways impossible to modern man, no matter how philosophical. Today a lesser thinker must hide in his Third Avenue pub and snatch a tough steak and worse potatoes to nourish him if he cannot bear to go home and face the sour woman he is commanded by law to live with. Indigestion is the inevitable aftermath, not so much from the rank victuals he has stowed away as from his basic sorrow that he and she have come to such a pass.

But if he does go home, his stomach will curse even louder, thanks to the acids of anger and hatred that he can counteract in the pub with aloneness and a couple of short ryes. He sighs, gulps, and looks over the bar at his own mirrored face, bitterly thankful that he does not see there the pinched, ruined beauty of his woman, the Sarah-Jane, the Frances, who forced him here.

And she? Women have more ways than men for lone survival, so Xanthippe may drink too much, or exhaust herself in a whirl of club meetings with her like, or sit weeping and moaning in a darkened movie house. She may long for her husband . . .

. . . and then when he does come home, heavy with fatigue and forced joviality, she forgets her longing and slaps ill-cooked food upon the table, a kind of visual proof of her boredom at his dullness and her hatred of his dwindled lust, which she, poor soul, was genteelly raised to mistake for love. She may even try hard to be patient, and not to mind when in subconscious pain at the sight of her sharp face he hides it from him with a spread-out sheet of news about pugilists and midget auto-racers. She may hope that he will notice the cherry she has, with synthetic optimism fed by radio commercials and monthly magazines, placed upon the top of his canned peach.

But he reads on, with the instinct of a cornered toad pretending courage, and in desperation the woman, who has sworn not to do it again, begins to talk.

The rest is too familiar, a pattern used tastelessly by comic-strip writers, modern literary giants, and psychiatrists: she whangs, he scowls back, suddenly the food in their bellies feels intolerably sour and dreadful, he returns in a furious rush to his pub and she to her bitter, teary pillow, and finally they end according to accidents of time and place and money in the relative asylums of death, insanity, hypochondria, or the law courts.

A good answer to this Xanthippean formula must start practically with the cradle. A child, male or female, who has been raised to eat in peace, and has never gulped to the tune of scolding or anger, stands a better chance of knowing the pleasures of the table when he is full grown than one who has listened with fright and final callousness to endless bitter arguments and rows, who has bolted his food to escape them, who has at last come to think them a part of family existence and to expect, with a horrible resignation, that his wife will turn out to be the same noisy, bickering shrew his mother was at mealtime.

I think that it is a good thing, for many reasons, to have children eat at least half their meals at their own table, at the hours best suited to them, and removed from sight or sound of older people whose natural conversation would be as boring to the young ones as theirs would be to their elders.

But if, as was true when I was little, the children must have dinner with their parents, some such rule as the one my family followed should be law: business was never mentioned in any way, nor money problems, nor grown-up worries. And if any of us children had grouses to air, or peeves, we did it earlier or later, but never at the table. There we were expected to eat nicely and to converse with possible dullness but no rancor, and, being expected to, we did—or else were excused from the room.

My father, because of the endless evening meetings he had to go to as a small-town newspaper editor, had to dine early, and my mother, dependent on unskilled "help," could not arrange separate dinners at different hours for the children and for herself and him, but I have often thought it a pity that they had to refrain from any of the rich quiet talk that a husband and wife should indulge in over their evening meal, in order to teach us children one more rudiment of decent living. The only place

where they could converse properly was in bed, and I can remember hearing their low voices going on and on, far after the
house slept.

Even so long ago I used to think how dull it must be for my
father to come home after the paper was off the presses and well
onto the streets to find my mother deep in the unavoidable and
noisy routine of getting four or five or six children washed and
brushed and ready to be fed, with never a chance to sit down together and breathe.

Perhaps that is why, now in my own life, I feel that the quiet
drink I have before dinner with my husband, after the children
have been tucked away, is one of the pleasantest minutes in all
the 1440. It makes the meal which follows seem more peaceful,
more delicious. Physically it smoothes out wrinkles of fatigue
and worry in both of us, which could, especially if we had been
conditioned differently by wrangling parents, lead us inevitably into the Xanthippean tragedy of nagging, and bitterness,
and anger. And that, I know because I have seen it happen,
would be the world's surest way to send my husband from my
table and my life—an ugly prospect indeed, and one rightly to
be avoided, just as is the poison it would take to do it, brewed to
the tune of a woman's shrewish voice and served, quick death to
love, at the family table . . .

I

. . . and it may be said here that no omelet can withstand the
spiritual battering of a bad-tongued shrew. It will look delicious, certainly, but turn to gravel between the teeth no matter
what its creamy texture or its fine ingredients.

I know how to make scrambled eggs that to my own mind
are, quite frankly, the best I have ever eaten, and they would
taste like old minced carpet and stick in my throat if I had to try
to swallow them while Xanthippe hacked at Socrates, or anyone else for that matter: a son, a relative of either sex. I have, in

public places, watched women suddenly turn a tableful of human beings into scowling tigers and hyenas with their quiet, ferocious nagging, and I have shuddered especially at the signs of pure criminality that then veil children's eyes as they bolt down their poisoned food and flee.

My recipe, guaranteed to gripe a man's vitals if served with hate, and to soothe him like pansy petals if set down before him with gentle love, varies somewhat with the supplies to hand, but is basically this, and, as will be evident, it is quirky:

Scrambled Eggs

8 *fresh eggs*	4 *tablespoons grated cheese, or*
1½ *cups rich cream (more or less)*	*finely minced fresh herbs, if*
salt, freshly ground pepper	*desired*

Break eggs into cold, heavy iron skillet, add cream, and stir gently until fairly well blended. Never beat. *Heat very slowly, stirring occasionally in large curds up from the bottom.* Never let bubble. *Add seasoning (and/or cheese and herbs) just before serving. This takes about half an hour—poky, but worth it.*

This concoction is obviously a placid one, never to be attempted by a nervous, harried woman, one anxious to slap something on the table and get it over with. Its very consistency, slow and creamy, is a deterrent to irritation, and if it were attempted by any female who deliberately planned to lean over it, once on its plates, and whang at her guests (for a lover, a husband, a father, or a child is indeed the guest of any woman who prepares the food they must eat), I would rather have my scrambled eggs turn into hard, fanged snakes and writhe away. I love this recipe, for its very gentleness, and for the demands it makes upon one's patience, and the homage it deserves from its slow tasting.

I can suggest a good recipe for a shrew, to take little time, be very indigestible, and imply frustration, outrage, and great boredom by its general air of hardness and tough, careless preparation:

---

4 *eggs*　　　　　　　　　　*cooking oil or fat*
4 *tablespoons water*　　　　*salt, pepper*

Beat eggs angrily until they froth. Add the water. Season without thought. Heat oil quickly to the smoking point in thin skillet, pour in egg mixture and stir fast. Scrape onto cold plates and slam down on carelessly laid table.

This is of course a travesty, rather grim, rather too recognizable. What usually happens with Xanthippes (and I have heard several of them confess to it, with a strange perverted smile) is that they "just open a can of beans, if Harry takes it into his head to come home on time for a change!" I have even heard some of them add, with a yet stranger smile of sadistic (masochistic?) bravado, "No fancy stuff! If he wants all the trimmings, he can get it from *her*!" (Or, "at the Brass Kettle!")

The recipe here is unprintable, but with merciful briefness I can say that it consists of one can of baked beans, one can-opener, one plate, and, as a special Lucullan touch, one cloggy bottle of old catsup.

Now I know myself to be guilty of many a sin, but I feel fairly safe in saying that Xanthippean gastronomy is not among them. And yet I confess to a great liking for canned baked beans, as well as to a sociological admiration for them and what they stand for. Perhaps the worst I ever ate were in a pub in Cornwall, the locality's fanciest, where an open can of them stood proudly at one end of the bar, surrounded by good honest slabs of freshly baked bread, as snacks for the regular patrons. Cold, sluggish, a hideous tone of mud-gray-brown, they were served forth to us by the publican as a true Yankee delicacy, and I gulped down my share with a rewarding glow in my soul for the interested friendliness of everyone around me, and no thought of the horrid taste and the texture of what I gulped.

Quite aside from any and all such sentimental connotations, I think American canned beans are wonderful. They are quite (and I use the word "quite" in its proper sense of "utterly," "completely") inferior to home-prepared beans, which send out from a winter's oven a warm, rich smell unlike anything else on earth. (My mother used to put a pot of them on the farthest-off ledge of the furnace for five days or so, when she was a bride in Michigan, and her father-in-law would say gently, chopping his way down to the edible parts, "A peck of charcoal a year never hurt a good man, my dear.")

I have a fine recipe for them, in which the beans must cook gently, covered and in the slowest oven, for at least eight hours, and which toward the end, say a couple of hours before supper, should have hot bacon drippings poured drop by odorous drop over their top crust. It is, indeed, fine.

But I can also make a good thing out of two cans of ordinary beans—like any woman who will consent to earn her just reward by the happy palate rather than the acid tongue:

Beans

2 or 3 No. 2 cans pork and beans, any reputable brand	1 teaspoon dry mustard (or 3 of prepared)
½ cup molasses, "black strap" if possible	6 strips sliced bacon or ½ cup melted bacon drippings

Mix beans, molasses, and mustard thoroughly in generous casserole or baking dish, put bacon across top or dribble melted fat evenly over it, and bake in moderate oven (350°) until bacon is almost crisp or top is crusty. Serve with toasted sourdough bread (or steamed Boston Brown Bread if you must), and crisp celery . . . and beer.

Y *is for* Yak

. . . and the steaks that may possibly be carved, now and then, by hungry visitors to the plateaus of Tibet if they can sneak one of the great black oxen far enough from its native owners . . . as well as for other peculiar steaks, stews, and soups which have nourished men, for one reason and another, within my own knowledge.

To be truthful, I have never met anyone who would admit to tasting yak. Perhaps these bisonish beasts are too valuable as vehicles to end in the pot. Perhaps there are religious scruples against devouring them, as with the sacred cows of India. Perhaps it is simply that I do not move among the gastronomically yak-minded.

But whale, now: I can discuss whale, at least vicariously enjoyed. I was married for a time to a man whose father, a most respectable Presbyterian minister, once spent a large chunk of the weekly budget on a whale steak and brought it home gleefully, a refugee from respectability for that one day. Who can know how many memories of unutterably dull prayer meetings the exotic slab of meat wiped from his mind? It may well have been opium, moonlight, orchids to his otherwise staid soul.

Whatever the escapism of his purchase, it threw his harried wife and his four habitually hungry children into a pit of depression. They had no idea how to cook it, and stood looking helplessly at it, wishing it were a good honest pot roast.

What finally happened to it completed the dismal picture: it was treated as if it were indeed chuck beef, and the minister, his wife, and the four children ladled off cup after cup of blubber oil, which rose high in the pan for hours while they waited, futilely, for the meat to grow tender enough to eat.

It was possibly the first, and certainly the last, attempt the minister made to flee from his proper routine of prayers and pot roast, pot roast and prayers.

The only successful dish of whale I know about was the result of a Machiavellian plot, carried out quite successfully too, by more or less Machiavellian but certainly hungry people. To begin with, a young oceanographer was given a piece of whale by the captain of a hush-hush government ship, which, it may be deduced, had been exploring far northern waters. This was in the deepest days of meat rationing, and the oceanographer brought home the great slice of ruddy meat with both pride and jubilation.

His beautiful blond wife admired it properly, but she was a scenario writer, not an Eskimo, and the three cookbooks she owned said nothing, less than nothing, about what to do with whale. She was very resourceful, however, and her quick brain lit upon the fact that a producer-friend had lately married a Hungarian girl who was supposed to be able, and indeed could, make two old riding boots and an onion into a dream dish—given plenty of paprika of course.

The whale steak went into the oceanographical laboratory "cool rooms," the producer and his new wife were invited for the next weekend, and, the blond writer added casually, "We have a simply fabulous and fantastic surprise for you!"

The Andrássys, for such was approximately their name, drove hungrily down the long coast on Friday after the studios in Hollywood closed, he thinking, "Food! I am starved for something that doesn't taste like lunch in the Commissary and dinner at Mike's!" and she thinking, "Food! I am starved for something I never saw before, something I haven't had to buy and cook, for other people to rave about."

The whale steak, but lately removed from the lab, so that it was stiff as a granite cemetery stone and of almost the same gray color, lay on the kitchen table as the supreme welcome to them.

The next few minutes have never been described to me by my well-mannered friends, at least not to my satisfaction, but the end of the evening is very clear. It seems that some five hours after the Andrássys arrived, and bolstered by beneficent libations, they and the blond scenario-writer and the oceanographer sat down to a truly delectable and beautiful dish, which, naturally, tasted exactly like Hungarian goulash, complete with paprika and without a trace of whalishness about it. Even Mrs. Andrássy enjoyed it.

There is a creature something like a whale, for he lives in the cold northern waters as whales often do, and something like an elephant, for he has two ivory tusks, one of which grows long and curved and handsome. He is called a narwhal, and although fewer men have tasted him than have tasted either whale or elephant, his skin is reported to be delicious, crisp as celery and tasting of nuts and mushrooms—and looking like half-inch thick linoleum, which for me at least would prove an esthetic handicap.

As for elephant meat, many human beings have enjoyed it, mostly in jungles, but also, it is admitted, within walking distance of the local zoo. One man I know who was the most skilled butcher in his district had a standing agreement with the zoological gardens near him that he might do a bit of sub-rosa carving "in case of accident" to any of the more exotic guests, and he assured me over several bottles of Tavel that elephant trunk is one of the most succulent meats ever swallowed (except perhaps crocodile).

Certainly some such menu of the Siege of Paris in 1870 as the one which can now be seen at Voisin's in New York is ample proof of the gruesome legend that Castor and Pollux, the two elephants of the zoo, ended nobly in the soup kettle after everyone in the city who could afford to had supped from them.

The Voisin menu, to celebrate Christmas on the ninety-ninth day of the Siege, is an unpleasantly fascinating example of what people will eat if they are hungry enough. Besides the consommé d'éléphant it boasts stuffed donkey head, roasted camel, kangaroo stew, rack of bear, leg of wolf, cat garnished with rats, and antelope pie—a far cry from the first timid use of anything extraordinary *chez* Voisin, when Bellenger consulted with his chef and grudgingly devised a menu around the meat course of saddle of spaniel!

The degree of exoticism is dictated by both time and place, of course. One winter in Strasbourg I ate wild boar as if it were commonplace beef, but in Southern California I would feel strange indeed to find it set before me. And when I was a child I dried kelp leaves over our evening beach fires and ate them happily, quite unconscious of the fact that probably nowhere else but along the shores of northern Japan were children doing likewise, and all because my Aunt Gwen had been a child there herself and was now helping to raise me in the only pattern she knew.

I have always believed, perhaps too optimistically, that I would like to taste everything once, never from such hunger as made friends of mine in France in 1942 eat guinea-pig ragout, but from pure gourmandism. The first time I ever felt this compulsion of gastronomical curiosity over instinct was when I was about fourteen and was confronted with my first shrimps. (I do not understand how it took me that long to meet one; perhaps my grandmother's rigid Midwestern ideas of what was fit and proper to put on the table kept me from that pleasure.)

I was immediately repelled by what now delights me, and the little curled pink things, lying in whorls upon the mayonnaise, with snow packed around the bowl as only "Victor Hugo" could do it so long ago in hot Los Angeles, seemed horrible to me. I looked about the airy charming room, with the canaries singing in their golden cages and soft lights glowing behind their incredibly fancy chiffon shades, and I recognized the fact that I was facing a test: I must eat at least one shrimp, and *then* die or be sick.

It was the first of uncountable more, from many a bay and stream, of every color from dank gray to rose, every size from bee to field mouse. Once I saw a corpse fished from a Louisiana bayou, and it was three times its size for the shrimps sucking at it; and another time I saw another corpse, off Brittany, stripped by lobster claws; and still I think without any qualm at all that shrimps, and all their cousins, make one of the sweetest things in this world to put between my teeth.

The next hardest test I passed, at table, was my first oyster, an overlarge and rather metallic one, in the dining-room of The Bishop's School in La Jolla, a few years after the shrimp.

I found it dangerously disgusting for several minutes, but since that memorable day I have eaten oysters whenever I could, including one very bad one in Berne which, my husband told me, would prove to have been all right if I did not die within six hours. I did not, although the last hour had me waiting with ill-concealed anxiety, my eyes on the clock and one hand lying expectantly upon the bedside bell.

I later learned, from no less an authority than Henri Charpentier, that the best thing to do if a bad oyster has been swallowed is to drink generously of coarse red wine, whose tannic content will counteract the acid in the rotting mollusc. I have never had a chance to prove this, I add almost regretfully, for since I learned the trick I have not been in oysterish places.

Imagination tells me that probably the hardest test I could face would be to eat live maggots which had lived in a cheese, like the dish Charles Reade wrote of in *The Cloister and the Hearth*. But I am quite sure I would try, without too much squeamishness, the white termites in Africa, which must be snapped at skillfully before they bite the tongue, and which, more than one gastronomer reports, taste very much like pineapple. For some reason the thought of them does not repel me, nor, at least theoretically, does the story of the tiny live fish which are swallowed by some South Sea tribes during feasts, to flop around in their bellies and make room for more food.

As for roasted locusts strung on twigs over a fire and basted with camel butter, I think they sound very good indeed, since I react well, gastronomically, to things that are crisp and not sweet, and I might find them almost as irresistible as my peak in this category, the potato chips in the bar of the Lausanne Palace, which were hideous to any kitchen purist, tasting one time of chicken fat, another time of lake perch, but so fresh and so crisp and so salty that ten years after I last ate one I can enjoy it still, and will ten years from this present vicarious enjoyment.

I have found that people, when questioned about the strangest things they ever ate, are vague, and I myself am so. One man to whom livers-and-lights are anathema will say that the worst experience he ever had was finding himself halfway through a grilled kidney before he realized what he was eating. Another will go dreamily into the story of the time William Seabrook picked up what was presumably an oxtail bone and announced to his well-fed guests that it was the best human coccyx he had been able to buy for a long time. Personally I can murmur no such ghoulish titillations at the proper or improper moments. But although none of my acquaintances has eaten yak, one man I know, who has become a bishop, told me, long ago, of the time he went to a savage Oriental village and was served, by the head man, a stew of what he knew at a glance was boiled new-born baby. The Christian pretended to eat it, feeling souls at stake, and later confessed he was not overly relieved to learn that it was little monkeys, not children, he had nibbled at.

So, limited as I am to shrimps, oysters, and wild boars, I still do talk with people, now and then, who have known stranger flavors: monkeys and crocodiles, the ordinary whale, the extraordinary innard of a calf.'

I

To many a man who has never heard the forthright British term "offal" in connection with livers-and-lights, they are still just that.

Gastronomical prejudices have a fleeting vagueness about them, a mysterious, shadowy equivocation. If you ask anyone why he shudders away from grilled calf's liver, he will murmur a seemingly haphazard excuse, usually drawing, to prove his point, on childhood shock, racial traits, and what his grand-mother told him once. And yet he purrs like a happy cat when confronted with a fine jar of truffled liver pâté! Or if you de-mand a reply to your question about his almost pathological horror of kidneys, the most direct thing he can say is that he re-fuses categorically to eat a critter's innards, and then wonders why he isn't served smoked tongue once in a while!

(This happened to me not long ago, and my fastidious but confused friend was more than annoyed, indeed almost in-sulted, by my bland remark that a calf's tongue is as much a part of his innards as his brains, cheeks, head, heart, kidneys, liver, muzzle, palate, sweetbreads, and those enigmatic delicacies known to some Western cattlemen as "mountain oysters."

(Indeed, I added cruelly, even an ox tail can be considered as what a *nice* butcher calls "a tidbit." My friend turned gray-green, as heavy prejudices, acquired God knows where and how, made all the delectable soups and stews heave dangerously in his spiritual belly. I formed, and then as quickly discarded, a pettish resolve to serve forth no oxtail stew until a fine skewer of kidneys and tomatoes had been pronounced bliss rather than anathema. But why fight? Such inner battles are part and parcel of a lifetime's story, and perhaps one more facet in the jewel's perfection.)

I know of countless ways to make nourishing and delicious dishes from kidneys, tripe, brains, and yet not only must I not serve them in my own home for reasons of marital stability, but I could not buy the supplies in the village near us if I needed them, because I would be the only person for miles around who would countenance having them in her house.

Even here in the United States, where most hundred-per-centers don't know tête de veau exists, and if they did would be horrified by it, there are dozens of good cookbooks with dozens of good recipes for such extraneous delights. But butchers say sadly that more and more shoppers, young and old, seem incapable of ordering anything but lamb chops, sirloin steaks, and an occasional roast.

I don't know what the answer is. Quite aside from such unreasonable and intrinsic prejudices against sweetbreads and kidneys and such as I can recognize in many of my friends, there seems to be a powerful combination of snobbery and culinary laziness that makes most cooks avoid them. And since an increasing number of people do their own cooking, the prospects for eating a good cervelle au beurre noir or tripes à la mode de

Caen a half-century from now look very slim indeed. I myself need not worry overmuch about the gastronomical pleasures of that far time, but stubbornly I could wish to prepare my children for them.

The only gesture left to me is to pass on to them, from a great sheaf, one of my favorite recipes. The very mention of its main ingredient sends their father grimly from the room. I copy it secretly, rather as a prisoner whittles at his cage, rather as if it were to be a tiny sign, fifty years from now, that hunger for more than T-bone and French fries gnawed at one woman's gastronomical consciousness.

It stems (all my pet rules *stem*) from a page of Ali-Bab:

Kidneys Ali-Bab-ish

2 pairs fresh kidneys	salt, pepper
3 tablespoons butter	1 cup thick (or sour) cream
brandy	1 teaspoon horseradish sauce
sherry	(optional)
1 cup sliced mushrooms (fresh or canned)	

Slice kidneys nicely and brown in very hot butter (this is a good chafing-dish recipe). As soon as brown, set aflame in glass (about ½ cup) brandy. When flame dies completely, add same amount good dry sherry. Add sliced mushrooms, cover, and simmer about 10 minutes. Season to taste and add the cream (and horseradish if desired). Bring quickly to boil, then serve on crisp toast (or with rice).

Z *is for*
Zakuski

. . . and for a few reasons that I think a discussion of hors
d'oeuvres is a good way to end an alphabet as they themselves
are to begin a banquet.

The main trouble with them, almost a legendary one, is that
if they are enjoyed to the hilt, the meal that follows is, can be,
and usually must be more or less ignored—except by real
trenchermen, that is. The variety, the tempting spicy smells,
the clashing flavors, all lead even jaded appetites to a surfeit that
destroys what is to follow, no matter how simple or how Lucullan.

Gastronomically this may well be thought a pity, at least by
the sad hosts who have commanded a feast thoughtfully and
then found their balanced courses almost painfully shunned by
their too satisfied guests. Even so, it is fun now and then to roam
uninhibited and unhurried through a smörgasbord, a buffet
russe, hors d'oeuvres variés, however it may be called. Myself,
I like the name zakuski, although I don't know why, for I have
never had them in the classical way, countless bowls and dishes

and platters set out upon a long table, to be tasted as and how I wished, and swept down with frequent little glasses of vodka.

The nearest I came to that was when I used to go to a small cellar-restaurant behind the Russian Church in Paris, after Sunday morning services. I always stopped in the bar and drank one or two vodkas and ate pressed caviar, the black at about eight francs if it had been a flush week, the red at five francs if it had been a thin one.

And I felt much too shy to go into the next room where everyone standing around the long table was speaking Russian with a liveliness that to me still seems part of the zakuski ritual. I remember how thin most of the people looked, and how handsome: that was not long after Paris had filled with refugees from the Revolution, and although I was innocent of the average American awe at having princes for taxi drivers, I could not help admiring the way most of the people in the café-cellar held their heads.

I do not know quite how they paid for the things they nibbled so avidly and gaily: whether there was a flat fee for this little post-churchly spree, or whether some sharp-eyed waiter totted up their various mouthfuls. As I say, I was too timid and too far out of my lingual element to investigate, and instead stayed in the bar, absorbing by a kind of gastronomical osmosis the high spirits in the other room.

My time was far from wasted though: I learned the lasting delight of pressed caviar, which I found to be best when it was most removed from freshness, when, in fact, the barman hacked it off the mother lump as if it were a piece of rubber, and it had to be chewed and mumbled over in the mouth. Then it went down in a kind of gush of pureness, caviar in essence.

One day I staggered into the bar, dizzy from the most beautiful a cappella singing I had ever heard in my life or in my dreams, and the barman, who by that time recognized me, put down before me on the counter a tough slab of the red and a little brimming glass, and for an instant I felt very lonely and wished that I might be in the other room, where people milled merrily after the strain of standing and kneeling and then standing all morning. But next to me I suddenly saw a big man drinking vodka from a water tumbler, and he too was eating pressed red caviar, holding it like a slice of bread in his hand, and he was joking with the barman. Something about the vibrations of his voice made me recognize that it was Feodor Chaliapin who spoke, and that it had been he, no other in the world, who had sung in church that morning with the choristers.

I must have looked the way I felt, awestruck and flabbergasted and naïve, for the barman said something and they both glanced at me and smiled, and then Chaliapin clicked his glass against mine and said, "*Santé!*" and they went on talking in Russian.

It was a strange moment in my life, as strong and good as the taste of caviar on my tongue and the bite of vodka in my throat. I walked straight out, past the door to the other room, where the gaiety and the countless zakuski no longer lured. Everything was in shadow beside the almost brutal glare of the voice that had so uplifted me in church and then had said "*Santé!*" to me. Even now I blink a little, spiritually, thinking of it.

Caviar, of course, is only one zakuska. (Personally I think it is the best one and would willingly forego almost any other gastronomical delight for it—*enough* of it, which I have never had, even though once I slowly and happily ate a pound of it by myself, over a day or so in time and unlimited distances in voluptuous space.) It has for many centuries been thought the most luxurious of all hors d'oeuvres, too good for ordinary diners or dinners. Even Shakespeare used it as a simile: "Caviare to the general . . . ," he wrote in *Hamlet* about a play which pleased not the million—and indeed it is reported that British soldiers stationed on the Caspian Sea after one of the last wars complained angrily about being fed too much of "this 'ere fish jam."

I moan at the thought and wonder if they would have liked any better the lowest form of it, a futile imitation called Peasant Caviar, made of eggplant and various seasoning. I myself think it utterly delicious, no matter how far removed from what it tries to counterfeit, and would gladly eat it spread thick and cold upon black bread every summer noontime of my life. It is another zakuska, seen more upon poor sideboards than rich ones, of course.[1]

Then there are all the pickled mushrooms and tomatoes and eggplants, usually flavored with dill in one degree or another; and the pickled smelts and boned pickled anchovies, the smoked salmon and sturgeon, the little fried or poached cheese pats called tvorojniki, the pirojki stuffed with a dozen things like game, fish, cheese, cabbage, mushrooms; and bowls of mushrooms in sour cream; and, of course, the vodka (this and tequila are the two most appetizing fire-waters in the world, I think, although I learned from one of Arnold Bennett's books to find good dry gin a fortunate substitute for either of them).

That, all that and much more too, will make an honest side table of zakuski. Anything that follows is incidental, obviously, although at Easter time, in Russian households all over the world of whatever political hue, it is obligatory to stay upright if not completely sober for the main table of baked ham and ducks and suckling pigs, and the high baba and the cone-shaped paskha, and the painted eggs all nested in their grass and blossoms.

A man I know who spent his boyhood in St. Petersburg has told me that never in his life, anywhere else in the world, did he see such Gargantuan, near-insane gourmandizing as on Easter at his home, when he was about twelve. He cannot forget it, nor how the still merry people fell back like walruses into their chairs, for the gentlemen had visited several other houses for a nibble of the special zakuski and a nip of vodka, and then had met with their women and children at his parents' house for the rest of the traditional celebration. He shakes his head now, with a half-incredulous, half-envious look in his eyes that says, too recognizably, There were giants in those days. . . .

I have never seen such a rite, raised as I was prosaically if with less digestive danger in a small California town, but I remember the first time I ever went to the Brasserie Universelle in Paris, which was notable then for its hors d'oeuvres variés, a great favorite with provincials like me. I was young and hungry, with a commensurate capacity and sturdy bodily functioning. I had never beheld so many tempting dishes in my life, and the waiters who brought, in a seemingly endless procession, hot, cold, spiced, bland, scarlet, green, black things to set before me apparently enjoyed my pleasure.

"Hold back," one would advise tensely. "Wait! There will soon come a truffled pâté one must taste!"

Or another would say, "Now just a tiny little morsel of this, it is not too distinguished, to save place for the cèpes which are next."

And so it went, I sitting back in happy helplessness, like a queen ant being nourished by her husbands, feeling myself grow great with sensuality.

As I remember, this happened several times, only by virtue of my youth and general good health, and at the end of each meal I toyed languidly with a Coupe Jacques. I could face neither the hors d'oeuvres nor the dessert today, but it is somehow pleasant and reassuring to feel that I was not always thus ascetic, and also that I have known more exciting things than the tray of canapés which is considered the American equivalent of zakuski, in whatever language it is said.

What emasculation they have undergone, these pretty and

minuscular appetizers! What a far cry, no matter how artfully made and served, they are from the generous bowls and tubs and boats of a buffet russe, a smörgasbord, a table of hors d'oeuvres variés! And for that matter, how far from the straightforward and tonic thrust of vodka or aquavit is the genteel stimulation of no matter how fine a Sidecar or Manhattan, the vulgar and happy wallop of even the best Martini!

I cannot ponder upon a Gargantuan Easter in St. Petersburg, but I can succor my hungry memory with thoughts of pâté and mushrooms and suchlike in an upstairs restaurant in Paris; and perhaps better than any of this with thoughts of the simplest zakuska ever eaten, when Feodor Chaliapin ate it too and touched his tumbler to my little glass.

What better way could there be, to begin a meal or end an alphabet?

I

Peasant Caviar, somewhat ironically named in my opinion (I have known a few so-styled *paysans*, but never any who either could afford to or would want to make such a mishmash), can have its own strata of richness, extravagance, and giddiness. I know and use three different recipes for it, depending on both my purse and my patience, and I suppose that whoever makes it has a somewhat different version from any of mine.

They fall roughly into the following kinds: (1) cheap, easy, and refreshing; (2) fairly expensive and finicky; (3) expensive, dark, rich, and fancy-fine.

The first I keep in a covered jar in the refrigerator, a kind of private restorative which I usually manage to do away with single-forked for lunches, and perhaps some Ry Krisp but more often nothing at all. It is not pretty, but like many another dish of whom and/or which the same has been said, it is good:

Number One

1	large or 2 small eggplants	½	chopped fresh green pepper
1	minced onion		(optional)
1	mashed garlic clove	¼	cup fresh herbs chopped (also
1	peeled chopped tomato		optional)
	or	3	tablespoons vinegar
½	cup tomato sauce or catsup	3	tablespoons olive oil
			salt, pepper

Boil the unpeeled eggplant in ample water until tender. Cool, peel, cut into small pieces, and stir vigorously with the rest of the ingredients, added slowly, until it is a well-blended mush. Chill well for at least a day before serving. Use with thin black bread as an appetizer, or as an accompaniment to cold meat.

The second recipe is perhaps the best of the three, but I am too lazy to make it very often. It was taught me by a Honey-colored Actress along with a lot of other gastronomical jewels. It is, given her strange patience, perhaps more like real caviar than anything could or should be, because the trick of slow baking disposes of much of the vegetable's pulpiness and leaves only the dark little egglike seeds.

Number Two

Put three or four mature eggplants in a pan (they will dwindle astonishingly) and let them stay all night in the lowest possible oven heat, around 225°. In the morning scrape the pulp from the withered and blackened skins and put it, and any black juice that may have accumulated, into a big bowl. Beat strongly as you add minced onion, garlic, herbs, seasonings, and vinegar and olive oil, rather like a salad dressing. It should be a heavily flavored mixture, according to your own tastes and distastes. Put in a cold place for at least 24 hours before serving.

The third rule is a fruity concoction, to quote my father. It is rich in color and texture and a little overpowering in flavor, so that it needs crude black bread to be eaten with it, and vodka or jolting Gibsons or some such drink alongside it. People who have been in Algeria and Turkey and such localities say they have often eaten something that looks and tastes pretty much the same.

Number Three

1 large onion	½ cup (scant) good vinegar
4 tablespoons olive oil	salt, pepper
2 small or 1 large eggplant (about 6 cups, cubed)	2 tablespoons oyster or Worcestershire sauce
2 cups diced peeled tomatoes *or*	
1 cup tomato sauce	

Chop the equivalent of about 1 cup of onion, brown it well in the oil, and add the peeled, cubed eggplant. Stir carefully until nicely brown. Then add the tomato, the vinegar, and the salt and pepper. Mix well. Cover and simmer for about 1 ½ hours, stirring occasionally. Add the oyster or other hot sauce, mix well, and allow to cook slowly with the cover off until it begins to look thick and dryish. When the eggplant is thoroughly done, remove from fire, beat well, and pack in jars, to store in a cool place for at least 24 hours.

A chapter about hors d'oeuvres at the *end* of a banquet book might just as well retrogress one step further and make its final bow with a short and appropriately dry discussion of what has become the American equivalent of vodka, aquavit, and other such whips to the human appetite: the Martini.

The first one I ever drank was strictly medicinal, for threatened seasickness, and in spite of a pure enjoyment of them, which may be increasing in direct ratio to my dwindling selectivity of palate, I must admit that I still find them a sure prop to my flagging spirits, my tired or queasy body, even my over-timid social self. I think I know how many to drink, and when, and where, as well as why, and if I have acted properly and heeded all my physical and mental reactions to them, I have been the winner in many an otherwise lost bout, with every-thing from boredom to plain funk. A well-made dry Martini or Gibson, correctly chilled and nicely served, has been more often my true friend than any two-legged creature.

On the other hand the tipple can be dangerous, and I, when about to drink one, make sure of several things, but mainly how soon after it I can expect to sit down to a decent bite to eat. If things look grimly as if they would drift on; if my host has a glint of predinner wanderings and droppings-in in his eye; if my hostess seems disarmingly vague about how to get a meal on the table; if all this obtrudes no matter how quietly into my general enthusiasm, I firmly say no, to no matter how masterly a mixture of gin, vermouth, and lemon zest.

If, on the other hand, I see plainly that I can relax, confident of tangible nourishment within the hour, I permit myself the real pleasure of a definite alcoholic wallop.

There is no less vulgar way of expressing what a dry Martini gives me. It is as warming as a hearthfire in December, as stim-ulating as a good review by my favorite critic of a book I have published into a seeming void, as exciting as a thorough buss I have yearned for from a man I didn't even suspect *suspected* me.

There are two classes of non-professional Martini-makers, those who are rudely convinced nobody in the world can make one quite as well as they, and those who shy away from the bar and say with melodramatic modesty that they can ruin *any-thing*. The second, when pressed, usually make much the better drink.

My own rules for Martinis fall, like those for Peasant Caviar, into three somewhat loose groups: the safe, the perfect, and the intimate (and therefore pluperfect).

The first is the mild kind I give to people I don't know well, which means, truthfully, that they are not close enough to me to betray how many or what kinds of drinks they have had before they knock on my door, and that I want to serve wine with the dinner I have carefully prepared for them and do not care to have them turn mussy and maudlin and monotonous. It is made of two parts of good gin to one of dry vermouth, and is stirred with ice, poured into chilled stemmed glasses holding not more than two ounces, and served with a green olive stuffed preferably with a pearl onion but passably with a bit of pimiento or almond-meat, and the oil from a twisted lemon peel on top. It is mild, generally safe enough, and can be very good.

The second type is the one I ask for on my occasional sprees in the region's best restaurant, wherever I am. If I do not know the barman, I try a single Gibson. If it is good, I know that I can ask for a double one with equanimity, and from then on not bother with the first puny sample known as a bar drink. (I was raised to accept Gargantuan glasses as my just due by my extra-tall, extra-lusty father, and I am incapable of feeling that anything but a double-sized drink is potable in public places.)

Given the fact that a barman understands what I want, I like, then, on my rare and deeply savored debauches, to precede the luncheon or dinner with one double Gibson, to be served to me in a chilled champagne glass, with the lemon peel twisted once lightly over it. My favorite Bacchus gives me a little dish of salty pearl onions, impaled properly on tiny sticks, lying in a bed of snow. I never touch them, but we respect each other for this sop to custom, a compromise on his part with putting onions into the drink itself, and on mine with wishing that they not appear at all.

Perhaps the best bar Gibsons I ever drank were made by a

man in Colorado Springs, in the old Antlers Hotel, I think.
They were about four parts of gin to one of vermouth, and after
stirring them he put a tiny spoonful of the pickled-onion liquor
into each portion. I have tried this, but I suspect that the so-
called cocktail onions we have produced, since war made life
"so dreadfully difficult" for us drinkers, do not have the correct
Dutch kick to them. Certainly the trick has not worked any too
well for me, which is one reason why my second category of
Martinis is arbitrarily professional, and why I myself no longer
try to duplicate what Bacchus can so deftly and beautifully flick
before me.

The third kind, which I have dubbed intimate, is something
which should never be served in public, nor to any but the one
or two people you know best in the world. It should never be
drunk when weariness or the moon's tides or the press of
worldly business are too evident, nor when red wine is to follow. But given an easy, airy evening, a pleasurable quitting of
the day's chores, and the prospect of uninterrupted and peaceful
communion with One, it can be a fine thing indeed.

My recipe sounds like a parody of Robert Benchley's apoc-
ryphal dictum which electrified early Martini-bibbers: three
parts of gin and enough vermouth to take away that ghastly watery look. Mine says four parts of dry gin and one eyedropper
of vermouth! It must be served very cold indeed, in generous
wine goblets, and it is, in truth, a version of what is still much
better than *it* can ever be, for such things: vodka, aquavit, tequila. . . .

It seems improbable that my hint of herby wine, the tonic
quality of a drop of vermouth, could possibly turn straight dry
gin into a quick-working apéritif, but it does: chilled gin has
nothing in common with this ridiculously delicious cocktail,
and unless it be colored with a drop of bitters, or poured from a
cold stone flask of real Geneva, it is a poor way to precede a

meal. Given the silly fillip of a scant driblet of vermouth, icy-cold gin can make a private and soul-satisfying drink indeed, and one not to be indulged in lightly, too long, or oftener than the stars dictate.

It is a special thing. It, like other more subtle assaults upon our senses, can bring peace with the pain, and a kind of surcease, gastronomical and therefore spiritual, from the world's immediate anguish. Palliative or poem, it is good.

From A to Z

THE PERFECT DINNER

Once while I was walking in a leisurely but not dawdling way from Vézelay to Avallon (it was only about sixteen kilometers, but I managed to spend a good five hours covering the gentle empty roads), I discussed, with an intensity seldom given to any conversation and very rarely sustained without boredom for so long a time, the subject of The Perfect Dinner.

Everything was in favor of such a quietly passionate entertainment. The weather was heady, an April day of breathtaking clearness after days of rain, so that the earth steamed and quivered a little in its pushing fertility, and birds in the air and hares along the ground and moles and earthworms underneath it sent out an almost tangible excitement. I myself was young but not too young, healthy and free-limbed. And my companion was not only my true love, but also a man I knew to be the most charming talker in a world largely peopled by the stiff-in-tongue, so that quite apart from our shared physical emotions we could speak together, tirelessly, any time at all, of no matter what, and find it good.

All this conspired to make our nonsensical deliberations on The Perfect Meal as celestially enjoyable as such communion possibly could be, and although I have by now forgotten most of what we did decide upon, the slow steady murmur of our voices, thoughtful one minute and mocking or purely silly the next, echoes unquenchably in my mind's ear. It was a kind of contest, and as we walked on and on toward Avallon we fought with all our wiles to win, one from the other, the palm for perfection.

We decided, after some fumbling and confusion, that time, place, weather, and, above all, people, were as important to the gastronomical consummation as the food itself. We settled on six as the perfect number of guests, including our two selves of course.

I remember that I named Colette (I might not today, feeling that in her powerful old age she would monopolize the conversation, never a good thing at such a feast as I wanted then and can still dream of), and the Prince of Wales (whose impossibly attractive person had not yet been dimmed in a million women's minds by Mrs. Simpson's svelte shadow and who, I thought, would, because of his great social skill, make a proper table companion, amusing if not witty, charming if not overly intelligent). I cannot remember what two other people were my guests, nor any of my love's, and I have forgotten every other detail of his plan, which by mutual agreement won the palm from mine.

I know that I wanted my meal to be served at the cool end of a hot August day, while there was still light in the sky for the first part, with candles to come later, on a wide studio-balcony on the top of a house on the Quai Voltaire in Paris, the whole glass wall of the apartment open that night, with dusk-colored gauze curtains moving faintly in the air rising upward from the Seine, and the pink lights of the Tuileries coloring the sky. (That is all I wanted!)

Food I have forgotten, except for one detail I insisted on, enthusiastic even so long ago in my belief that unexpectedness and a modicum of astonishment enliven any good dinner: I stipulated one course of small, fairly peppery enchiladas, using real tortillas and slivers of chicken breast, obviously a prodigal version of this delicacy but coming fortuitously at the end of the hot, enervating day—or so I thought then, and still suspect.

And that is all that is left in my conscious mind of the long, solemn, ruminative discussion—all that can be made tangible. Colette has withdrawn, and so has the Prince, and so, even further, has my good companion. And I am less capable of nonsense and find reality easier to think upon, more probable. I can still plan perfection, but I am impatient of not attaining it, where on the road to Avallon I could contemplate any fantasy with seriousness.

It seems to me now that for my own satisfaction I must divide Perfect Dinners into three categories, none of them too improbable. And I need not depend, as I did that far day, on perfect synchronization of the weather, the place, the décors; time's passage has made me willing to compromise a little.

I feel now that gastronomical perfection can be reached in these combinations: one person dining alone, usually upon a couch or a hill side; two people, of no matter what sex or age, dining in a good restaurant; six people, of no matter what sex or age, dining in a good home.

Three or four people sometimes attain perfection either in public or in private, but they must be very congenial, else the conversation, both spoken and unsaid, which is so essential a counterpoint to the meal's harmony, will turn dull and forced. Usually six people act as whets, or goads, in this byplay and make the whole more casual, if, perhaps, less significant.

The six should be capable of decent social behavior: that is, no two of them should be so much in love as to bore the others, nor at the opposite extreme should they be carrying on any sexual or professional feud which could put poison on the plates all must eat from. A good combination would be one married couple, for warm composure; one less firmly established, to add a note of investigation to the talk; and two strangers of either sex, upon whom the better-acquainted diners could sharpen their questioning wits.

All six should be congenial in their vocabularies—that is, they should be able to converse in one or more commonly understood languages, and the words they use should be neither too simple nor too elaborate for comprehension.

As for social hurdles, they should not exist, but if by chance one otherwise intelligent and charming guest would, because of early training or later worldly compulsions, prove incapable of dining with pleasure in the company of a butcher or a nuclear physicist, the latter should be invited some other time, or vice versa: it is ridiculous to threaten an evening's possible perfection in the name of democracy, gastronomical or otherwise.

Some such dinner party, then, for six carefully chosen people, should not be given in a public place: a large table in a restaurant, unless it is isolated in a salon privé, is awkward to serve and to manage conversationally. If the noise of the other diners is heavy enough to cover the sound of six people's talk, it is also loud enough to reduce all the talking to twos. And if a subject is interesting enough to lure the six into discussion of it, their voices will be forced to a shout that is unattractive and in the end uncomfortable. No, six are too many for anything but a private room, and a family dining-room, no matter how ornate or simple as long as it is fairly small, is the best place.

There they can be served easily and smoothly by one servant or by the host or hostess. They can attain, in the intimate quiet, an effortless familiarity impossible in public. They can spend as long or short a time over every course as their pleasure and the spiritual climate dictate, without thought of the unavoidable rhythm of restaurant service. They can also, and this is perhaps most important after their basic congeniality, eat dishes impossible to command in no matter what large kitchen, things shunned by busy professional chefs for reasons of snobbism, economy, or unadulterated ignorance.

It is advisable, to my mind, to avoid serving foods that are too exotic, too highly spiced; one of the less familiar guests may be actively nauseated at the mere mention of escargots à la mode de Bourgogne, or be sent toward death's door by a Bombay curry. On the other hand, I think it a pity to serve a sirloin steak, no matter how good: that has become almost an obligatory order, nine times out of ten, when people go to restaurants as a routine thing.

If beefsteak is to be eaten, it should be in some such incredible form as tournedos Rossini, which hardly any chef will bother to prepare properly (if he can afford to), and which will please the guests by its luxurious unexpectedness.

If chicken, perhaps the second-most-ordered food in public eating places, seems indicated for whatever reasons, it should not be fried or roasted as any restaurant will present it: it should remain chicken, plainly and honestly, and comfortably recognizable in order not to scare away the skittish; if fried it should perhaps be placed with mushrooms in a casserole of cream, and if roasted it should perhaps have a dressing never tasted before by any of the guests, of kasha and minced clams.

In other words, the usual should be made unusual; extraordinariness should cloak the ordinary. So long after my decision to serve enchiladas on a Paris roof to Colette and the Prince, I still believe firmly in the attributes of the unexpected! I still believe, perhaps stubbornly but with a satisfying list of proof to back me, that hidebound habits should occasionally be attacked, not to the point of flight or fright, but *enough*.

A guest, for instance, who boasts (stupidly or not as it may seem) that he is a meat-and-potato man, should be given just that. But the meat should be a little gigot of lamb, with a clove of garlic tucked into it and a quick douse of brandy and flame to cut the sticking fatness, cooked in an almost tepid oven until the juice runs clear, and no more. A casserole of peas and mushrooms would walk in with it most happily. And the potatoes? They'd follow, making the next course noble and alone, beaten until cloudlike with cream and butter and then piled into a dish, dusted with Parmesan, and put for one moderately searing moment under the oven flame. The meat-and-potato man would thus have his accustomed fare, but just enough out of focus, standing just honestly enough on its own various pedestals, to astonish him, and please him too, if the cook had St. Teresa on her side to admit that God walks among the pots and pipkins as well as in the cloisters and the marts.

A meal which might be perfect for six well-chosen guests to enjoy and linger over in a small room amply candlelit would perforce depend upon the hundred aspects already hinted at, of place, weather, temperament, and such. Hunger and fair-to-good health are basic requirements, for no man stayed by a heavy midafternoon snack or gnawed by a gastric ulcer can add much to the general well-being. Given, then, six people (two beautiful, one intelligent, three of correlated professions such as architecture, music, and photography); a cool autumn evening with perhaps enough wind outside to make the dining-room sound more like a haven than usual; a good cook . . .

I am that all-powerful being, tonight at least, with Black Bea in the kitchen to cope with the order I fight for but do not always maintain. I have slyly kept last-minute preparations to their minimum, so that I appear uninterested in anything but my guests. We have Martinis or sherry before we enter the dining-room, and red caviar in a generous bowl, it being easier to be generous with the red than the black or gray just now. There is thin dark bread, with a pat of sweet butter and cut lemons; no hidden economy of chopped onion, chopped egg, to stretch out the primitive goodness of the taste.

The dining-room table is set with warm colors, this being autumn: reds, brown-handled knives, strong plates and sturdy goblets, pink and purple grapes in the center—a very blunt decoration indeed.

First we drink a hot consommé double, of equal parts of clam juice and veal stock, to carry the fish taste over to the coming meat taste, and laced with dry vermouth instead of sherry to interrelate the Martinis and the wine to follow.

That will be a firm, rich Burgundy type, too heavy for anything but celebrations, in this case a Paul Masson Pinot Noir, standing three bottles deep on the sideboard, handsome indeed in its thick green-glassed pomposity.

Next comes an almost medieval platter of rump roast baked artfully with prunes and then smothered in a sauce that might be dubbed sweet-and-sour by the unknowing. It falls under the knife in hearty slices, and there is a casserole of wide noodles in butter, to go with it and take up some of the heady juices.

The wine flows down happily. The six people talk, move with a new ease upon their seats and in their skins, feel a new zest, Breughel-ish.

Then there is a large but bland green salad ("to scour the maw," Rabelais would say), made with the minimum of good wine vinegar so as to leave unassaulted the strong tannic impact of the wine, and gently toasted sourdough bread, which stays on the table for the next course of a hand-count of cheeses on a board: buttery Gorgonzola, Camembert "more running than standing," impeccable Gruyères, Cheddar with a bite and a crumbling to it, and double-cream as soothing as a baby's fingertip.

The wine improves, especially in the third bottle. The candles begin to flicker. There is bitter black coffee, sitting carelessly beside the last bits of cheese, the last freckled crumbs of bread upon the cloth. There is, above all, a kind of easiness, which at this point in my life, both social and private, I find more valuable than rubies, for waily-waily, too often now the world's woes press in like a tumorous growth upon our hearts, like a relentless balloon upon our tables, like a sword upon our beds. If, in the alchemy of hospitality, some such ease as I have told of may be attained, it is to our general good and devoutly to be wished for, and while better, wider-traveled wines and rarer viands might be substituted for my menu based on local possibilities and my own purse, no happier result could follow, to my thinking.

The question of what to do with four people is a different one, and as I have already said it depends dangerously upon the keen mutual interest of the four. It can too easily turn into a business conference or, in the case of two men who meet for dinner together with their doxies, a complete rout. When necessary, it should be held in private.

Two people who dine together are a different thing again. They separate themselves into two more kinds, the ones in love sexually and the ones in love.

In the latter class I think of myself dining with my father, such a strangely relaxed, amicable meeting after the years of family confusion at table; of several meals I have had, at noon and at night, with women who for one reason or another attracted me—their brains, their creamy cheeks, the way they talked about their lovers; a dinner in the back room of a shoe repair shop with the cobbler, the two of us in a kind of gastronomical communion, tasting and sniffing without a thought of the sheets that are supposed to cover invisibly any such male-female encounters: I was in love with all these people, and richly rewarded for being so.

But the other kind is more demanding. It can and should be

disciplined. The best place to indulge in it, when two people are sexually caught and still must eat, is in public, granted of course that they are well in hand and able to observe the amenities of combining such a basically physical act with the one they already have committed, may soon again commit, and now wish they were committing. Anything else is unthinkable, and I dislike the memory I have of countless couples mooning at each other over good food gone to waste.

I think a delicately chosen, artfully presented, lingering, and languorous meal, indulged in publicly, can be one of the most successful fillips to a love affair, but only when it is done with some intelligence. The presence of the other near-invisible diners makes the promised isolation seem even more desirable. The waiters float in a conciliatory cloud. The food—but there is no need to give details of that in such an amorous pattern: almost anything in a good restaurant will be tinder to the flame, breath blown on the ash.

The love feasts that perhaps need, and merit, more thought, are the ones between father and daughter, mother and son, sister and sister. My reason for making these rendezvous apparently adulterous is that in a proper family its various members seem able to attain an easiness of soul together, not known by most other people. But I have lunched once with my literary agent in an airy women's club in New York; I have sat once on the chair that Somerset Maugham had just stood up from, and spent three hours there, beside a beautiful woman who was my husband's wife before I was; I have been with a lanky, handsome secretary in a Hollywood Strip restaurant eating cottage cheese and fruit, which I loathe—and always I have reached a peak of contentment, satisfaction, fulfillment, which is a special virtue of sharing food in a public place with one other human being, of no matter what sex, who for that moment at least is naturally close.

Perhaps the most limited, and at the same time most intricate, form of the perfect dinner is the kind eaten by one person. Then food takes strange forms, and so indeed does the position it is eaten in.

Where in a restaurant with his loved one a man might order his accustomed pattern of oysters and a dry Riesling, little roasted squabs to nibble at with wild rice, and a watercress salad with chilled fruit to follow, a Château Neuf du Pape and brandy of the best, alone at home he will lie back in his deepest chair, a low table handily beside him, and eat a series of unforeseen concoctions.

One man may want a cold plate, and upon it a cold, topless tin of salmon—no mayonnaise, no toast, no nothing—and a stiff Scotch and water. Another may putter and simmer over his electric hot plate and produce a strange dish of tinned shrimps, slighty blinky cream, wilted scallions, and too much tabasco, which he will pour happily over a piece of yesterday morning's toast and eat languorously, one hand holding the latest pocket edition of *Blood Fell on the Corpse* and the other piloting his fork to his mouth with deep satisfaction and a feeling of culinary triumph. There may be anything from Pilsner-Urquell to the tail end of a bottle of Wente Mourestel in his glass, and indeed drinking is something of an interruption in such a feast.

Then again there is the studied, deliberate dining alone, not accidental but arranged for in a kind of purgative sense, which I and most other thinking people (I use the word "thinking" in a nonphilosophical but gastronomical connotation) have practiced.

I figure that the peace and requisite relaxation of sitting by myself in front of a little fire, or in a shadowy patio in summer, are worth the effort they take, occasionally. They are in a way a kind of retreat. I balance my day to their accomplishment. I arrange them as if I were sending a posy to Jenny Lind, with all the proper bows to protocol. Finally I am there, alone, upon a chaise longue, or a tuffet. I have, according to the season, my mete and proper meat.

In the winter, if I am indeed alone, I drink some *good* vermouth, which seems increasingly hard to come by, and eat a little thinly sliced smoked salmon (this is a dream, of course, winter or summer), and then a completely personal and capricious concoction, shrimps or lobster tails or chicken in a thin, artful sauce, very subtle indeed, the kind that I like to pretend would be loathed by anyone but me. I eat it with a spoon and fork. I have a piece of good toast at hand, but hardly touch it. And I sip, from a large, lone Swedish goblet, all its mates being long since shattered, a half-bottle of well-chilled fairly dry white wine; there is something delicately willful and decadent about drinking all alone no matter how small the bottle. And then, after one ruminative look at the little zabaglione I have painstakingly made for myself sometime earlier that day (I enjoy desserts in theory, but seldom can come to the actuality of eating them), I close the refrigerator door firmly upon it and go to bed, bolstered by books to be read and a hundred unattended dreams to be dreamed.

The slightly depraved ramifications of dining alone are plainly limitless. I have savored many of them and do not feel myself the loser. In the main, though, I prefer the category of Two: a white-maned literate male who is past wanting me, a beautiful woman who would not want, a man who would . . . above all the company of One other, making the rarest kind of Two . . . and for lack of that, granted that in my own time I can gracefully eat alone if I am meant to do so, I would choose, at spaced deliberate intervals, the excitement and the whetting, the conflict and the intricate patterns, of a perfect Dinner for the Six of us.

Index of Recipes